Abounding Grace

By the same author:

Abounding Grace

A Meditative and Devotional Study

by

NORMAN PITTENGER
King's College, Cambridge

MOWBRAY
LONDON & OXFORD

Copyright © Norman Pittenger 1981

ISBN 0 264 66789 1

First published 1981
by A. R. Mowbray & Co Ltd
Saint Thomas House, Becket Street
Oxford, OX1 1SJ

Computer assisted photo-typesetting by
Elanders Ltd, Corby, Northants, NN17 1BP

Printed in Great Britain by
Richard Clay (The Chaucer Press) Ltd
Bungay, Suffolk

Contents

Preface

Friends and acquaintances have often told me that they would like to read a simple, direct, and experientially based discussion of the familiar phrase 'the grace of God.' Far too many discussions, they say, are too theologically oriented and often phrased in language that the ordinary man or woman does not understand. And they have gone on the express their opinion that God's grace, perhaps more than any other religious concern, is in fact appropriately presented in a straightforward fashion, since after all it has to do with God's working in us, with us, and for us, in concrete human experience.

In this book I have sought to respond by writing about grace in its various aspects so that its practical relevance may be grasped. Above all, I have urged that grace is nothing less than God's love acting humanwards. We know it 'experimentally', as John Wesley said; and it can only be 'proved' – or tested, as that verb originally signified – in what his brother Charles called our 'experience' of it.

To speak of God's grace as 'abounding' is exactly right, for it is God's gift which we can never merit and never earn but must always receive in wonder and gratitude. Somebody once said that 'grace means glory'; God's glory is disclosed in his gracious action, claiming us, asking our glad response, and humbling us to acknowledge our unworthiness to receive it, yet gratefully saying our little 'Yes' to its marvellous working.

NORMAN PITTENGER

1

What is Grace?

SUMMARY: *Grace is not a thing given by God. It is God himself as he acts lovingly and faithfully with and in his world. We are enfolded in this grace, even if we do not always recognize and acknowledge it as such.*

'Grace' is a word that appears innumerable times in the New Testament, above all in the letters of the apostle Paul. And in the prayers and worship, as well as in the thinking and writing, of the Christian ages, it is a word that is used with such frequency that probably we may say that very few religious terms are so often employed, yet so little understood, as that word 'grace.'

'The grace of God', 'the grace of our Lord Jesus Christ', and similar phrases are familiar enough to us all. But what do we *mean* when we say them? Often enough, alas, they are only conventional bits of religious jargon, whose significance has not been explored. But surely this ought not to be the case. Any term which has so long a history in Christian life and thought should be given careful consideration, in an effort to grasp something of its richness and understand something of its importance. This short book is an attempt to do just this. It is not a biblical study, such as might be appropriate in other connections; neither is it a theological exploration, such

1

as would be entirely proper in an intellectual connection.

Rather, it is intended to help the Christian disciple, man or woman or young person, to see something of the richness, something of the significance, to which we have just referred.

Grace is not a thing

One of the difficulties which we face at the very beginning is that people have sometimes talked as if grace were a *thing*. An old prayer, found in the English and other Anglo-Saxon Prayer Books, speaks of God's 'pouring his grace into our hearts.' Certainly such a way of speaking suggests a 'thing' idea of grace, as if it were a liquid which could be poured from one container into another. But we who are Christians cannot, or at least we should not, talk in 'thing' language when we speak about God and his ways in the world. Somebody has said that it is a mistake to talk about God as if his language was nouns or substantives; the right way to do this talking about God is in verbal fashion – which is to say, God is one who *acts*, who *does* things. *God's* 'word' is God's deed. Unlike us, he always speaks in what he does. Whereas we tend to speak in propositions or sentences or statements, our heavenly Father speaks to his children through his activity in loving-kindness, in his judgement through what happens in the world and to them, and by means of his forgiveness and mercy shown in the events of their lives as they are brought to respond to his insistent and unfailing doings towards them. Grace, then, has to do with divine action.

Still another difficulty in much that is said about grace is the way in which some people regard it as only a 'working' of God, so that it may be sharply distinguished from God himself. A popular hymn by John Henry Newman suggests that God's 'presence and his very self' are different from his grace. It speaks of that grace, in

2

relation to God himself as found in Jesus, in these words: 'And that a *higher* gift than grace Should flesh and blood refine; God's presence and his very self And essence all-divine.' But surely this is wrong. Theologians say rightly that God is *simplex* – all of a piece, so that his nature, his essence, his attributes, and his activities are one thing. If that is the case, as surely it must be (for we are not polytheists, who believe in more than one God, nor are we those who divide God up into pieces made up of 'this' and 'that'), then to speak about grace *is* to speak about God himself. As N.P. Williams, an Oxford theologian of the earlier years of this century, insisted over and over again, God's grace is nothing more, and nothing less, than God himself at work in the world and among his human children. So it is itself 'God's presence and his very self and essence all-divine'; it is not something apart from, or different from, that divine reality.

Many years ago a Christian thinker who was writing about St Augustine and his teaching, incidentally remarked: 'For Augustine grace is the divine love in action'. (Kenneth E. Kirk in *The Vision of God*). This thinker was making a highly important point; but it is too bad that he did not put his insight in another way – although he may have intended it to be understood in that other way. He *ought* to have written that grace, for St Augustine and for any other sound Christian exponent of it, is *God* in action. Why do I say this?

God's grace is his active love

I say it for the simple reason that I take with utmost seriousness the great text of St John in his First Letter: 'God is love.' To say that God is love is to affirm that the divine reality from whom all comes and to whom all goes, the supreme 'dependability in creation' (as an ancient hymn-writer in the Church's early days once phrased it), the 'disposer supreme' of all things (as still another

3

hymn-writer of that early period said), is nothing other than 'pure unbounded love.' Far too often people have thought to honour God by using of him grandiose language more appropriate in the court of an oriental dictator or despotic king. Or they have described him in language which would suggest that he is primarily a moral governor. Or they have spoken of him as if he were an impersonal principle, such as 'being itself' or 'prime substance' or 'the reality upon which all depends.' All talk of that sort, however, misses the significance of God's own disclosure of himself through the history of the Jewish people, of which the Old Testament is the record, and in the event which we call 'the advent of Jesus Christ', to which the New Testament is witness. In the Bible there is a movement of human interpretation, responding to a movement of God towards his human children, which reaches its climax and consummation precisely in awareness of the truth given in 'advent' of Jesus Christ.

The meaning of it all was grasped and magnificently proclaimed when St John, and in other words and ways St Paul too, dared to assert that *love* is the reality behind everything.

God was preparing his human children to grasp just that truth and then to live in terms of it. It was a long preparation, for men and women were not ready at first to accept it in its startling challenge and in its reassuring reality. But 'in the fullness of the times' Jesus came; and in him that truth, challenging and reassuring, was acted out on the stage of history and in human experience. At long last, the fact was made plain; and John states it in that simple text: 'God is love.'

God's love is strong

Now we must be careful, of course, when we use a word like 'love' with reference to God. Perhaps especially in our own day, when love is so often taken to be only sentimentality, niceness, easy acceptance of anything and everything, with no biting-edge, the danger of misunderstanding is very real. Love in the New Testament sense is indeed accepting, but it is also demanding. It is generous but it is also exacting. It is wonderfully kind, but it is also inexorably stern. Thus when we say that 'God is love', we must understand that we are very far from speaking of him as a sentimental, rather silly, easily tolerant, kind of being. Rather, we are speaking of him, in language drawn from our own best experience, as one who is both gracious – and here we come back to the word 'grace' used of God's activity – and also severe. C.S. Lewis wrote to some friends about 'God's severe mercy'. What a splendid phrase that is!

But if all this be true, we can then see why (as I said) Kirk ought to have said that grace is God in action, for grace *is* love in action – and God is love. If anybody were to ask us one day, what is distinctive about the Christian 'model' or picture of God, surely our answer would have to be that it is to be found in the fact that this 'model' or picture is given us in Jesus Christ who is 'the image of God', as the New Testament tells us. So a familiar Christmas hymn dares to say that 'Love came down at Christmas, Love all-lovely, all divine'; and it makes just that assertion – although of course the word 'lovely' has unfortunately come to suggest, in our day, something rather sloppy. It need not do so, however, since originally 'lovely' meant 'lovable' and 'attractive', as now and again it can mean even today. But it remains the distinctive Christian assertion, from which we must never turn away, that in our Lord Jesus Christ 'Love came down' – and because this is so, our 'model' or picture of God is one that portrays him as the *cosmic Lover*.

I write 'cosmic Lover' because it is important to stress that the love that 'moves the sun and the other stars', in Dante's grand words at the end of *The Divine Comedy*, is univeral or all-embracing in scope and concern – hence *cosmic*; and it is also particular and personal in expressing that scope and concern – and hence *Lover*, since love always personalises and particularises, dealing with each one in his or her special situation and with his or her special need.

To sum up what has been said so far, grace is not a *thing*, nor is it some working of God which is separated from his essential being. These are the two fallacies into which so many seem to have fallen and which must be resisted with all our strength.

'Kinds' of grace

Unless this is done, we shall be likely to revert to the old habit of making still further and even more highly artificial distinctions about 'kinds of grace', so that the unity of the divine activity in the world is lost sight of and forgotten. Of course, there is a sense in which one can make distinctions and speak intelligibly about (for example) God's 'prevenient grace', coming before any creaturely response and indeed making that response possible. So also there is a sense in which 'habitual grace' and 'actual grace' may be mentioned, the former having to do with God's continuing gracious action and the latter with the specific moments when he is *seen* to be acting with gracious concern for his children. And one could go on, to talk of 'baptismal grace', the grace given in the Lord's Supper etc. But this is only a theological distinction, however important that is. It has little interest for the ordinary Christian disciple. The point of the matter is simply that in any and every instance we have to do with ways in which God as love delights to move towards and work for and in his children. The various conventional discriminations are, as I have suggested, largely artificial, however convenient they may happen to be. It is as if we attempted to analyse out and talk separately about each of the many various ways in which some loved person or

6

friend behaves towards us. Thus we might say that now he or she is acting to awaken our response; now it is a case of coming to our help in some specific emergency; now it is merely the ordinary loving concern which is shown us every day of our lives. To talk in that manner would not be so much false as it would be very nearly ridiculous. This is not how we commonly think and talk of our friends or loved ones in their relationship with us.

Nor do we make sharp distinctions between those friends or loved ones and their ways of dealing with us. Rather, we speak of John's or Mary's loving us, in all our various circumstances; and we are grateful to them for their graciousness towards us. So it should be, should it not, when we speak of God and *his* attitude and action towards us? What it comes down to, indeed, is that we need to 'personalise' our talk of grace. For we are persons-in-the-making and God is the originative personal reality who is above us, around us, with us, and within us, unfailingly present and unfailingly at work.

What is more, God in his gracious movement towards us is not dependent upon our conscious recognition of him and his care. Somebody has said that much of God's doings in the world are 'anonymous', in that they are not immediately identified for what they truly are. This is an important insight. There have been times when devout Christians have mistakenly seemed to think that the reality and effectiveness of the divine working was dependent upon its being known as such – and then *we* become the central point, as if God's very existence would not continue unless we could indicate precisely that he was there. That is absurd.

Christian God-centredness

Several years ago a clergyman friend of mine told me of a little incident which demonstrated how easily devout people can fall into this man-centred position. He was greeting his parishioners at the church-door, he said; and one of them remarked to him; 'Your sermon this morning seemed blasphemous to me.' Startled by the comment, my friend asked in what way he had thus been guilty. The reply came, 'Why, you said that God would exist and would care for us, even if we did not acknowledge him!' But surely that parishioner's attitude reflected a quite unconscious but none the less serious blasphemy on her part. She was making God, so to say, an adjective modifying herself as a noun. That is, she thought of God as a function or quality of human feeling or thought, rather than as one who is always himself and upon whom *we* depend – not the other way round. Thus we can make the mistake of thinking of graces dependent upon our own recognition or reception of it, rather than seeing that this recognition and reception are awakened by, and dependent upon, the God who is gracious. We need to be theocentric, God-centred, in our thinking; we must avoid anthropocentrism, or man-centredness, as the blasphemous thing it is.

So we should see that grace is no thing separated from God but which God is pleased to give us. Neither is it different from God himself, as if we could divide or separate what God is from what God does. Rather, grace is God himself in action in his world and for his children. Further, because God is sheer love, in all its kindness and mercy but with all its demand and severity, grace is that very reality of divine love in action. This is why we can be assured that in any circumstance, wherever we may be and however we may happen to feel, we are loved by God and helped by God. His love, which is his 'very self', is present with us, active for us, concerned about us, ready to respond to us, anxious to work with us even before we have taken any steps towards him. His love, God himself *as* Lover, seeks us out, as the woman in Jesus' parable sought for the lost coin, as the shepherd searched for the lost sheep. His Love, God himself *as* Lover, comes out to welcome us as did the father in the story of the prodigal son, who embraced the wastrel for no other reason than that he loved him and wanted him back home with him in the happiness of the father's house and in the companionship of the father's family.

What has just been said will serve as an introduction to our discussion. In the following chapters we will concern ourselves with such matters as 'common grace', or God in the whole creation – a concept stressed by John Calvin but never absent from authentic Christian thought and experience; divine grace as found in the wider ranges of human experience and religious life; that same grace made distinctive and special through the coming of Jesus Christ; and the ways in which, through that grace, new life is made available to us in forgiveness, justification, reconciliation, enabling, sanctification, and finally in bringing us to genuine 'sonship' (or 'daughterhood,' as we should wish to add, in our own day) with the Father who cares, who cares so deeply that he will go to any lengths to win us to himself and to bring us to find joy in his presence.

2

'Common Grace'

SUMMARY: *One of the ways in which God acts lovingly towards us is in the natural order and in the world as we know and experience it. This is 'common grace', as theologians have called it. Thus God continually creates, sustains, and guides his creation towards the accomplishment of his purposes, making our lives meaningful and worth-while.*

When I was a theological student more than half a century ago one of my professors in the course of a lecture said something which I have never forgotten: 'It's natural for the supernatural to like to act naturally.'

At the time I was rather puzzled by this remark; but as the years have passed I have come to see the wisdom and insight which that professor expressed in those words. For while – to return to the theme of this book – grace is certainly a religious concept, it is not necessarily nor always apprehended and grasped in specifically religious ways. You do not need to identify any and each occasion of God's activity by *naming* him. A familiar hymn says that 'God loves the lowly spot'. And it is entirely in accordance with the divine humility and God's unwillingness to advertise himself blatantly and obviously, that he should work often, perhaps even generally, in a fashion which is not immediately recognized *as* his working.

I remember a rather stupid bishop, as I thought him to

be, who told his diocese in a pastoral letter that the United Nations Organization would never come to anything, simply because (as he put it) 'the name of God is not mentioned in its charter.' At the time when I read it, I believed that the statement was absurd. In fact, it seemed to me then, and it does now, to be almost blasphemous in its suggestion that God is so much like one of us, so arrogant and proud and insistent on being seen and respected, that he is quite the opposite of the disclosure made of him in Christ. In Jesus God did not announce in loud tones that he was present and active. Most of those who met Jesus must have regarded him as a Jew, doubtless a very distinguished Jew; it was not as if they could say, 'There is John the Baptizer, there is one of the scribes, and *there* in that Jesus is God himself.' No; the recognition of God's presence and power in his Son was and still is by the eye of faith. He is hidden *and* revealed there; he does not wear some placard which announces his deity. And so it is also with divine grace.

The divine humility

This patent truth may come as a surprise to us – or to some of us. We are so humanly conscious of our own supposed importance or of the importance attaching to other people that we find it hard to see that 'God's ways are not our ways,' any more than 'his thoughts are our thoughts.' We like to be seen and known of men, like the ultra-pious of the gospel stories who paraded themselves about the streets. But Jesus said that they were fooling themselves and trying to fool others. He said that it is in humility and self-effacement that God is appropriately worshipped and served. This is also the case with God's working.

Some of us find it difficult to grasp still another significant point. We have rightly and properly thought of God's grace as operating in our religious life and above all in our experience of redemption through Christ; but we can quite easily overlook his wider and more pervasive working in the whole of creation. We can think of God as being parochial in his activity, confining himself to what goes on in the sanctuary, in our prayers, and in our moments of specific religious feeling, thinking, and doing. But that is once again to make God after our own image; and it comes perilously close to the sort of anthropocentrism or man-centredness against which we warned in the last chapter. We can try to make God's grace simply a function of our own religious experience or faith, rather than see that it is the continuous and unfailing concern of God expressed in action, which awakens and then supports and augments our human response.

Some of Calvin's followers referred to what I have called, in the title of this chapter, 'common grace.' This is God's activity in the whole creation as such. Not only is he the originating one, the Creator (as we put it). He is also the one who upholds, maintains, and sustains all that is not himself. And since this is the clue to the creation as a whole, it is also the important point about every aspect of that creation. There is no absolute uncrossed gulf between God and his world. He is not a remote and for the most part absent deity who now and again makes an intrusive movement into that world. There have been people who talked like that. They were called 'deists' in the seventeenth century, to distinguish them from genuine 'theists' who insist that God is everywhere and always present in his world – although when we say this we must be careful lest we fall into the opposite error of *identifying God with* the world. On the one hand, God and the world are indeed different – Creator *and* creation – but they are not different in a way which would imply that there was not a constant relationship between them. On the other hand, God himself is with his world, yet not in such a fashion as would imply that he simply *is* the world. It is a matter of one thing present and working in another, as we might put it. Jesus himself, as he is understood in Christian faith, is our clue here. In him there are both God and man, both the divine and the human; but God is not a man, in a direct fashion; God is always God and man is always man. The affirmation of Christian faith is that God, while remaining always himself, acts in, and hence is present in Jesus through a genuine human life. This is what the traditional doctrine of the Incarnation seeks to assert. What is asserted there is true also – but not of course in an identical way, so Christians believe – of the working in which God in his grace is present and active elsewhere too.

But is not all this simply theological talk, with no practical implications for you and me as we try to live out our discipleship? Not at all. On the contrary, it is of enormous importance for our life as believers. Why?

God in the world

The answer is that we shall never be able to know that God is really with us in the moments of our religious life – in sanctuary and prayer, for instance – unless we have some glimpse of him in the world which he loves. Alternatively, we cannot know the quality or character of God unless and until we are able to see him in some one given place and time. The more general truth gives a grounding for the particular truth. The particular truth gives point and cutting-edge to the general truth. That general truth has to do with God's universal activity in the world which he not only has created and continually creates but also sustains and keeps going. Mother Julian of Norwich, a lovely medieval English saint, put this beautifully when she said that she learned from one of her 'showings' or visions that the creation *is*, 'because God loves it, because God keeps it', quite as much as 'because God made it'. That loving and keeping is by God's grace, his 'common grace,' active everywhere in the world.

13

As the reader is by now aware, we are discussing in this chapter – and in the one that will follow – this *common* grace, not the more vivid experience of God's working which we know in specifically religious existence and in our Christian faith. The use of the word 'common' is significant, for that word means general or universal or available for everybody and everywhere. The title of the Book of *Common* Prayer indicates that the services contained within it are meant for everyone, not for a special few. We speak of 'the common law', signifying by this a law which need not be spelled out in detailed and carefully defined ways but which is everywhere accepted and understood. So also we can talk of our 'common life', by which we mean the human existence which is found in any particular man or woman and which provides us with the assurance that ours is (again to use the adjective) 'a common humanity.'

In the next chapter our topic will be this common grace as it is known in the experience of men and women, even among those who are not in any conscious sense 'religious people.' But in the present chapter, our concern is with God's grace in the natural order. To speak that way may seem absurd to some people. For they have been told, often by scholars who claim to be 'biblical thinkers' but who seem never really to have read the Bible, that grace is to be known only in the realm of history and not in nature. Presumably the natural order is then irrelevant. At best, it provides a kind of back-drop or *mise-en-scène* for the events which take place in the realm of human history. But talk of that kind is not true to the general scriptural witness.

Some years ago, I heard a lecture by a distinguished teacher in a school for the training of Jewish rabbis. In the course of the lecture, the speaker said that the Jewish tradition knows nothing of holiness attaching to places but only of holiness as found in given times and persons. I was moved to put to him this question: 'How then do you account for the plain fact that in the Bible we read about "the holy land", about Jerusalem as "the holy city", and about the Temple there as "the holy place"?' I hope that I am not being unduly egotistic when I say that the lecturer was brought to a stop. He admitted that he had exaggerated, although he did this in his desire to make an important point about the central significance of historical events in Jewish thought. But his mistake, as I believed it to be, was typical of a certain kind of religious emphasis which in recent years has been altogether unfortunate. For it has failed to see that Scripture, above all the Old Testament, indeed emphasises the work of God in human history and in the affairs of men and women, but at the same time it stresses God's activity in the whole creation, not least in the heavens which 'declare his glory' and the earth 'which showeth his handiwork.' For the Bible the natural creation is the place in which God works out his purpose and it is dependent upon and sustained by him always and everywhere.

Reverence for nature

To understand and accept this must lead necessarily to an attitude of respect and reverence for the natural order. St Francis of Assisi spoke about 'brother sun' and 'sister moon'; and he esteemed birds and flowers and animals and everything else in the creation. He did not identify any of these with God himself but he did find God present in them and hence felt that they were akin to him in being (like him) 'creatures of God.' In our own time, and for many centuries past, forgetfulness of this fact had led to lack of reverence for God's creation, with the result in its exploitation and spoliation – to which nowadays ecologists are insistently calling our attention. The truth is that in failing to grasp the reality of God's working in the natural order we have tended to regard that order as simply there for our own convenience and use and for nothing else. But that tendency is based on an entire misunderstanding of the biblical imperative that we are stewards of the creation in its natural aspects – stewards are meant to tend, care for, and co-operate with that over which they are given stewardship. We are thus to be 'fellow-workers' with God in respect to the world of nature, not to be exploiters or ruthless destroyers of that world and its riches.

Science studies the natural order. It seeks to describe its regularities, discern its sequences, show 'how it works.' The job of the scientist is different from that which is proper for the man or woman who seeks God in that order, although of course there can be and there are many scientists who combine a genuine reverence for nature as God's handiwork with their scientific concern to observe and describe what they find there. Such devout scientists will sometimes say that they are trying to discover God's ways in the world; they speak wisely. Yet they must recognise that their scientific discipline is not the attitude of worship of God at work in the world which at other times and in other ways they feel compelled to adopt. It would be as inappropriate for them to introduce specifically religious categories into their experimental and observational labours as it would be to introduce scientific concepts and techniques into the worship of God in a church service. But they can show, as many of them do show, a genuine reverence for the natural world which they are also intent to study, although the way in which they show it is through their integrity, honesty, loyalty to the facts, and readiness to share with other scientists the results of their efforts.

Nor does the religiously committed scientist expect to find God visibly and obviously present. It was once said of Sir Oliver Lodge, distinguished British physicist of the early part of this century, that he seemed always to expect to discover God at the other end of his microscope. And we recall that a Russian leader said cynically that the astronauts from that country did not come across God as they explored outerspace. Evidently Sir Oliver was found to be disappointed if he did expect to see God through a microscope. Certainly the Russian astronauts were not likely to find him when they went up into the heavens above us. That is not how God works. As we have urged earlier, he is humble enough and wise enough not to disclose himself in any such simple fashion. God can be known only through faith, not by sight – whether that is the ordinary sight of mortals or the very highly developed sight made possible through scientific instruments or exploration. Yet he *is* known; and one of the joys of the Christian believer is to delight in him as 'manifested in his works' in the entire created order.

Our human response

Since all God's working is in grace, since indeed God's grace is God himself in action, we should then ask how we are to show our appreciation of this glorious reality in the natural world. The answer is that we are to show it in the way we look at nature, the way in which we use the resources which it provides, and the care with which we treat it. It has been suggested by those much concerned with our contemporary ecological crisis that there should be an eleventh commandment: 'Thou shalt reverence the non-human world and act in it and towards it with respect and concern.' There is wisdom in that suggestion. William Temple, a noted Archbishop of Canterbury, used to say that today there were very few more serious sins committed by men and women than the ruination of the natural order, for their own profit and pleasure and with no regard either for the integrity of that order nor for the generations which will follow our own and which (like us) will be dependent upon nature for the 'good things' which it makes available to us.

I happen to live in Britain, where rivers and streams

have been so polluted by the indiscriminate and selfish pouring into them of chemical waste that in many instances fish can no longer live in them. Americans are well aware of the horrifying way in which 'dust bowls' have been created through the reckless misuse of agricultural land, the careless destruction of forest areas, and the thoughtlessness so often shown by those who engage in 'scientific farming.' Not only are these a shocking misuse of nature; they are also, for those who believe that God is working to bring out the creative possibilities there, a blasphemous rejection of the divine purpose. This may serve to indicate a very practical response, to be made by faithful people, to the grace of God in our common human setting in a natural world which does not belong to us and which we have no right to spoil. One of the happier signs in our own day is the increasing awareness of human responsibility in this matter.

God's judgement

Such thoughts also bring us to see that while grace works for the good of others, it has also its hard or adamant side. The refusal to see and accept God's working can bring about dire results; those results are the penalty we pay for our selfishness, carelessness, and indifference. In this way, God's grace is our judgement, quite as much as in other respects it is our great benefit and resource.

A sentimental hymn found in some contemporary hymnals has in it these words: 'God comes down in the rain And the crop grows tall.' As they stand, those words are an expression of pantheism, which would identify natural phenomena with God himself. We have already seen that any such position is impossible for a Christian theist who must always insist that God and his creation are distinct one from the other. At the same time we have also seen that a Christian theist must recognize that God enters into, works through, sustains, and manifests himself in,

18

that creation. What the hymn is *trying* to say, but alas! fails to make clear, is that in the rain, when the 'crop grows tall', in the provision of the food we need, just as in the material which can be used for shelter and in all similar things, there is an activity of God which, like all his activity in every sphere, is indeed 'gracious.' God gives, generously and freely; it is for us to accept his gift with joy and thanksgiving. But it is *not* for us to use those gifts for our own entirely self-centred ends, regardless of nature and careless of other people.

Hence, when we talk about 'common grace', and by this intend the assertion that God is operative in the world of nature as also in human history and experience and in the 'saving grace' known in Jesus Christ and his redemptive work, we are at the same moment implying what ought to be our own attitude and action in respect to the natural world. We are implying, although this may not be so readily apparent, that failure in attitude and action in this as in other areas, brings with it penalties that are not to be escaped by pious utterances. What we *do* here is more important than what we happen to say on those occasions when we are consciously thinking about God and his grace towards us.

This judgement on us for our blasphemous disregard of one of God's signal gifts is not a judgement like a human expression of indignation or wrath. 'The wrath of God' is not an arbitrary and unreasonable explosion. It is part of the working of God in his creation. It is the adamant, stern, severe quality of his grace, which is never 'cheap grace'. That last is a phrase made familiar to many of us through the writings of Dietrich Bonhoeffer, the German patriot and martyr under the Nazis. By it Bonhoeffer was pointing towards an all too easy and undemanding view of God, as if he were a benign and silly father, and not the kind of father who expects, wants, and requires a responsible and authentic 'amen' to him in what he does and will continue to do. Thus there is also a profound truth in the words of the Swiss theologian Emil Brunner when he said that 'God's grace is our task.'

Brunner was saying this about the particular requirements that we respond in faith and obedience to God's action towards us, more especially in his redemption of the world through our Lord Jesus Christ. But his saying may be given a much wider application. Confronted by God's common grace in creation, living by it and dependent upon it, we are faced also with the demand which such grace makes upon us. That demand is for a zealous and highly responsible attitude and for equally zealous and highly responsible action.

I must leave it to the reader to think this through and come to see ways in which such an attitude and action can best be implemented in his or her own contact with the natural order, in support of the movement towards the rightful use of that order, and in readiness to protest vigorously against the exploitation and spoliation by which we so horribly distort and blasphemously mishandle what in his loving concern God has made available, and continues to make available, for his human children. The Psalmist prays that 'the earth may bring forth her increase and God may give us his blessing.'

There is one final consideration. Nature is often terrible but more frequently it is strikingly beautiful. We may think of the beauty of the sea, the mountains, the meadows, the glory of flowers and stars and the animal realm. One of the ways in which we can properly respond to this beauty is by seeing that in and through it something of the glory and beauty of God himself is disclosed to us 'through the works of his hands.' In the presence of such beauty we may well find ourselves compelled to fall down and worship – worship not nature itself, to be sure, but worship God who is *in* nature and who *through* it is calling us to adore him for his wisdom, his goodness, and his gracious generosity.

3

Grace in Human Experience

SUMMARY: *God's grace is not only at work in the natural world; it is also active in our human experience. God works towards us through our family, our friends, our human society, and all that 'builds up our common life', as Series 3 Communion Service puts it.*

We have been considering God at work in the natural creation through what we have called 'common grace'; now we turn to a consideration of God's common grace in relationship to human beings, the men and women who are the children of his love. Between these two there is a difference in what might be styled the intensity and directness of grace. In the former, the natural order at large, God is indeed present and active personally, since 'he is what he does', to use a phrase once employed in another connexion by the Anglo-American thinker Alfred North Whitehead. In the latter, in respect to men and women, he is also present and active personally, but with an intensity and directness which is more like our own relationships with one another than like those relationships in which we are acting (personally, of course, since we also are what we do) towards things with which we happen to be confronted.

21

A human analogy

This analogy may be pressed in order to make its point all the more evident. Let us suppose that I have a garden to cultivate. It is *I* who do the cultivating, so I am personally involved in the activity. Likewise, if I own a pet dog, it is *I* who own him, train him, and care for him. But it is a different matter when I concern myself, as I must, with my friends and neighbours. Again it is *I* who am in that relationship, expressing myself through my various actions towards and with those other people. It is even more a different matter when my relationship is with a member of my own family whom I love and for whose welfare, happiness, and growth I am deeply concerned. If it is proper to speak of 'human' grace – and certainly we may wish to do so when we consider how 'gracious' it is possible for us men and women to be in our human contacts – then we might well say that my grace expresses itself in one fashion when I am working in my garden or looking after my pet and in quite another, yet not entirely discontinuous, fashion when I am with my children, my husband or wife, my lover, or some other very dear person.

Of course this is an analogy and like all analogies imperfect, not least because it is human, with the defects, ignorance, and inadequacy which inevitably attach to human existence. But it makes its point, for it shows that even at that human level we are aware of continuity with difference. When we apply the analogy to God, we are able to see that while God is indeed personally concerned with, active in, and hence present through what goes on in the wider world of nature, yet his personal concern, activity, and presence in dealing with his human children is much more intensive, much more directly involved, and much more likely to vary as God adapts himself to the situations, circumstances, conditions, and needs of those human children. We have said that as the cosmic Lover God's sweep of concern is universal; we have also said that as a Lover, in all his divine glory, he acts always in particular ways with particular conditions. We can now go on to urge that God is one who knows what is in each of his human children, loving them as they are and for what they are. However much they may be sinners God loves them still, our Christian faith declares. But God also adjusts himself and alters his ways of relating himself to those men and women, in accordance with divine awareness of them in all their remarkable variety and with all their good and bad qualities.

God adapts himself

In specifically religious contexts, to which we shall turn in our next chapter, God's interest is to make himself known to his children so that they are enabled to respond fully to him in ways proper and natural to them. In the wider human situation, he works also to sustain and develop the best, since his intention is to bring those children to mature manhood and womanhood. He puts them in places and locates them at times in which he can promote just such maturity of growth. He does not do this in an arbitrary fashion as if he were a chess-player who moved about at will the pieces on the chess-board. To do that would be to violate the freedom and responsibility with which in their creation he has gladly endowed them. He does his work more subtly and wonderfully, by eliciting from them their own free response, as they answer to the lures, persuasions, invitations, and solicitations which press in upon them; and he asks them to decide for the right things in the right way.

Once again, the human analogy helps us here. A loving mother does not coerce her children to do what she knows to be best for them, even if on occasion she must use a certain amount of force to prevent them running entirely amok. More frequently, her way of bringing her children

23

to the maturity of manhood or womanhood, which she so earnestly and eagerly desires and works for, is by surrounding those children with opportunities to respond to circumstances in the sound and healthy way which will conduce towards exactly that maturity. To be sure, such a policy, with the actions which implement it in practice, is no easy matter to put into effect. It is a great deal more demanding upon her than would be shoving about and the use of sheer coercion. Patience, understanding, and readiness to forgive and act upon forgiveness, are now required. But any loving mother is glad to suffer the pain which is consequent upon adopting such a policy. She may be in anguish when she sees a child chosing wrongly and then being obliged to endure the results which follow from such a wrong choice. Certainly she will have to be patient as she waits for, and then delights in, the response which can take place. Yet she will know in her heart that the end-product is worth the pain which its attainment has involved.

God acts patiently

Like that loving mother, God acts towards us with enormous patience, with an understanding more profound and far-reaching than any human parent could summon up, and with the urgent desire that his children shall become what he earnestly, even desperately, wants them to become – which is to say to become full-grown men and women, who in responsibility make decisions that are in accordance with his purpose of love. Men and women are not treated by him as if they were things or as if they were slaves, but rather as his *children* who can learn to respond to life not in order to get what they want – and stop there – but in order to please their heavenly Parent. They can know that his will for them is nothing other, nothing more, but also nothing less, than their becoming creaturely, hence finite and defective, lovers who are

24

moving towards reflecting and acting for God's own divine and infinite love. This is surely a matter of divine grace. It is amazing grace; for what right have we to make any claims upon that sort of unfailing and indefatigable love?

How God provides

Let us now turn to some of the ways in which common grace makes itself known to us in ordinary human experience. There is no space here to list *all* of those ways, for they are as many as are the human beings with whom God is working. But we can suggest some of the ways; and I begin with grace shown in our relationships with friends and neighbours. That is an area with which we are all immediately familiar. Where would we be, how could we live as fully as we do, if we had no such friendships and no such neighbourly contacts?

All too often, alas, we simply take these for granted. But to do that is to be imperceptive. It would be impossible for us to be entirely alone, without the assistance and resources which such friends and neighbours provide for us. We depend upon them for more than we usually recognize. Not only in times of need, when we can turn to them for the help they may be able to offer, but also in times when we wish for and find a satisfaction of our need for companionship, we understand that the friends whom we know and the neighbours who are at hand make life bearable – more than that, they make life joyful and enriching for us.

Or again, consider our families. The Bible tells us that God 'has set the solitary in families'; and by doing so he has made possible intimate and enduring contacts which can bring sadness but are chiefly known for their capacity to bring us deep satisfaction and abiding happiness. A husband and wife, with their children, and all else that a family can give, find themselves fulfilled and their existence given depth and purpose. We yearn for such intimacy; and, thanks to the way in which God in his common grace has worked in the world, that intimacy is offered to us. It makes requirements of us, to be sure, as do our contacts of a less intimate sort with friends and neighbours. It is necessary to work at friendship and neighbourliness; in an even more intensive way, it is necessary to work at family life. But to say that is only to say, although in other words, that grace becomes our task. As we noted earlier, grace is not 'cheap', but includes both goodness and favour *and* demand with the requirement that we do our part in the situation. Family life and friendly relations cannot be at their best – in fact they are hardly possible at all – unless those who enjoy them are ready to give themselves, to exert their efforts, to keep them fresh, and to overcome the obstacles which so often might threaten if not destroy them.

Grace in social life

But there are also other ways in which grace works for the development of God's children. There are the situation and structures of human society. These include the regions in which people are brought together in common concerns, the various societies and organisations which offer the chance to work for the betterment of the community, and the many agencies and groupings that bring fuller life and promote welfare. Indeed any association of men and women who have shared interests can serve as a means of grace. We are often far too narrow-minded in assuming that the only means of grace are those which are obviously devoted to religious interests. But in the wider life of men and women in community there are gracious opportunities that should be grasped.

Still other secular 'means of grace' can be noted, in which concern for God's children is expressed in such apparently entirely secular ways as government and the state with police, fire protection, and the like. German Lutheran thinkers have called these the divinely ordained 'orders' in which human existence is both enabled and enriched. Whether we use this language or prefer to find other expressions, the truth remains that among the 'blessings of this life' are precisely such structures, apart from which or without which we could hardly exist in a human fashion.

Reference to such 'blessings' recalls the words of an old prayer in the Book of Common Prayer. In 'the General Thanksgiving', we thank God for 'our creation, preservation, and all the blessings of this life'; we then go on, very properly, to speak especially of our gratitude for 'the redemption of the world by our Lord Jesus Christ, for the means of grace, and for the hope of glory.' These last three phrases refer of course to the specifically Christian life, known to us in our being 'set right' with God through Christ, in prayer and the sacramental rites and ordinances which the Christian fellowship celebrates, and in the hope that God in his mercy will receive to himself those who have put their trust in him as he is disclosed in Christ. But notice that these quite evidently Christian moments are set in the context of God's creative and sustaining activity in nature (including what we discussed in our last chapter) and in his provision, by gracious working in the human world, of the 'blessings' to which in this chapter we are directing attention. The prayer does not say explicitly that these are also 'means of grace'. But it is entirely legitimate for us to extend that religious phrase to include the more secular graces which make our human living possible and which work towards making it *more* than possible, in fact towards making it as fully human, as richly and joyously experienced, and as rewarding for us, as human and finite existence will permit.

Thanking God for His gifts

All these can and should be included in our thanksgiving to God. The prayer makes that plain enough. Hence we may say that just as a recognition of God's common grace in the natural order brings us to adopt an attitude of respect, even reverence, towards that order and to act within it in a responsible manner, so also the recognition of God's common grace in our daily living one with another should bring us to be reverent towards others, thankful to them for what they give us, and concerned for justice and righteousness in human affairs. Through all this there should be profound thankfulness to the loving God who provides for us what we need in this life.

Practically speaking, we live with and by the help of other people and our very existence is made possible through the common life which we and they share. But much of the time we are forgetful of the ultimate origin of this help. It comes to us through human agencies and by human agents, to be sure. But in the last resort it comes to us from God who has so ordered the creation, both natural and human, that exactly these conditions are present. Once a year, on days set apart for thanksgiving – such as harvest festivals or American 'Thanksgiving Day' each November – we are brought to recognize this. We gather in our churches and we praise our divine Creator for his many and various gifts. Perhaps we include in that praise more than food and shelter. We ought *always* to do so, since even those things are given us by the labour of our fellow human beings and do not automatically make their appearance with no effort on the part of men and women. But in all this, and on every day of our lives, we who as Christians are believers in the God who is the final dependability and the ultimate origin of all that is good and right and true and healthy, should be grateful to the One whom an old hymn calls 'God the giver good.'

Human vanity and ingratitude

I have frequently been surprised and even shocked by the way in which so many of us, and I myself for so much of the time, seem to take all this for granted. I am appalled by the way in which we are even ready to assume that it is of our own making and hence is an occasion for proud boasting or arrogant claims to human competence and independence. Surely that sort of attitude is absurd once we come to think seriously about our life here in this world. It is also blasphemous since it is based on the all-too-selfish or egocentric assumption that we can exist in an individualist and worldly humanism which forgets God and focuses attention upon our own supposed achievements.

Ezra Pound in his *Pisan Cantos* wrote of human vanity, which he compared (not very fairly to the canine species) to a 'bloated dog beneath the sun.' He urged that we should 'pull down our vanity' and recognize humbly that it is not *we* who 'made nature' nor is it *we* who 'made grace.' Evidently he *contrasted* 'nature' and 'grace'; we on the other hand have seen reason to regard nature, in all its range including human nature, as a working of God's grace. Yet surely he is right in attacking the vanity which so mars our thinking and doing. What is demanded of us is a genuine humility. Humility will understand how God besets us round with, and generously provides for us, the good things and the human comradeship and help which we so much need. Having acknowledged God's grace in these ways, our further response should be thankfulness and praise. Without humility, with its accompaniment in gratitude and in adoration of the giver of all good, we become less and less human. On the other hand, humility, with gratitude and praise to God, makes us more and more human. We may then be led to be equally humble and generous in our attitude to others, equally prompt to assist them in their needs, equally glad to share in the common life which is ours, and equally prepared to spend our days, so far as we can, in the service of our fellows.

Thus what has been said in this chapter, has quite enormous consequences in the way in which we live. Above all for Christian people, who have received what St Paul called God's 'unspeakable gift' in Jesus Christ, there is the requirement that in *all* our lives, and for *all* our human circumstances whatever they may be, we give thanks to God who has made us and is always making us, who sustains us in existence, and who showers upon us his good gifts. As we have been seeing, these include family and friends and neighbours, human social groups, the possibility of living in an ordered and responsible way, and above all the love which we receive from others, unworthy as we are and yet needy as we are for just that love. That love comes ultimately from God, who is himself love and who would have his children live in love and act so as to make it more widely known and more wonderfully shared.

4

Grace in Religious Life

SUMMARY: *In religious life and experience, both Christian and non-Christian, something of God's gracious activity is glimpsed and something of his loving concern is known. He never 'leaves himself without witness'; it ought to be an occasion for joy, to realize this and to delight in it, wherever it is seen or discovered.*

We read in the Acts of the Apostles that when St Paul addressed the Athenians he told them that God had 'never left himself without witness' anywhere. And he took advantage of an altar in that city, with the inscription 'to the Unknown God', to make the point that the gospel which he proclaimed was about the God whom 'ignorantly [the Athenians] worshipped.' Throughout the succeeding Christian centuries the great main-stream of Christian thought has consistently affirmed that although God is distinctively and specially known in Jesus Christ, that same God has also spoken (as the Epistle to the Hebrews puts it) 'in sundry ways and in divers manners' to the Jews before Christ's coming *and* by implication to men and women everywhere. Hence, as Paul himself says in his letter to the Romans, all of us are 'without excuse' for our sinning, because all of us have known something about God and about his will for his human children.

Only in a very few Christian circles has there been a

narrowing of God's concern to the specifically Christian community. For the most part Christians have been generous enough in spirit to confess gladly that God is at work on all continents, among all peoples, at all times, and in many ways. Theologians have often talked of what is styled 'natural theology', by which they mean that by the exercise of the human reason something may be known about God: that he exists, that he is Creator, and that he is the moral governor of the nations. But perhaps it would be more appropriate not to speak of a natural *theology*, but of a natural *religious sense*, by which men and women everywhere can recognise something of the divine reality and in whatever fashion is possible for them can make some response to that reality in action in the world.

God with non-Christians

This is why it is blasphemous, to my mind, for Christians to think that missionaries in non-Christian lands are, so to say, introducing people to God as if such people had never known him in any way. Rather, I believe, we should think of these missionaries as concerned to give the right name to that God, proclaiming him as 'the God and Father of our Lord Jesus Christ' and showing by their words and deeds that thus to know God's 'name' – and let us here remember that for the Bible 'the name' is God's self-identification, just as your name and my name identify us for what we are – is to enter into 'newness of life' and to find ourselves put right with God, assured of the forgiveness of sin, and adopted in a special sense as 'heirs of God and co-heirs with Christ.'

There was a day when this deeply Christian approach to non-Christian people was not generally taken. Such phrases as the 'heathen in their blindness bow down to wood and stone' were frequently used. But St Paul knew better, for he saw and said that even in their 'ignorance' men and women were really worshipping the one and only

God there is. Although they did this imperfectly, sometimes even wrongly, and therefore stood in need of the saving gospel in which God has acted in Christ, enough was known so that worship *could* be directed in the right fashion and error *could* be corrected. At the same time whatever was right and true in such pre-Christian or non-Christian worship was corrected, crowned, and validated in Christ. A famous Indian missionary from Scotland once phrased this by saying that the coming of Christ should be interpreted to people of the great sub-continent as 'the crown of Hinduism', fulfilling earlier Indian religious awareness, correcting mistaken elements in that awareness, and making available for those people richness of life in Christ. Dr J. N. Farquhar, who used this phrase, was a dedicated and devoted Presbyterian missionary; his line of thought has been followed, although with considerable modification (especially of his idea about 'crowning' Hinduism), by the vast majority of men and women who have gone from what we like to think of as Christian lands to share with others the wonder and glory of the gospel of Christ. In Christ those others like us may find redemption and newness of life.

God's disclosure to everyone

I have said all this because I wish in this chapter to speak about God's 'abounding grace' in its wider expression through the pervasive and inescapable religious sense which is present in every part of the world and among men and women of many different cultures and traditions. But let me add here that this recognition of God's grace in such places and among such people need not and does not minimise or deny the speciality, the definitive and decisive quality of the gospel. It *does* make impossible for us the odd notion, odd surely for a Christian who believes that God is love, that this God is less generous than his human children.

A human analogy may help us at this point. I recall that some years ago when I was on a lecture trip in the United States, I ventured to remark that we could hardly avoid seeing that a great many, if not all, these active in the world of politics were 'scoundrels and corrupt men'. The reader may not agree with this judgement but that is what I said. In response someone said to me, 'Maybe what you've just said is true, but give us an instance.' It was the time of Watergate; so an instance and indeed some names were readily at hand and I gave them.

Thus it may be said in a similar way that the worship of the divine, in some form and through some mode of expression, is general throughout the world, yet we still need desperately to have a criterion, a specific and decisive 'instance', which will give point and cutting-edge to *all* human faith and worship. We need a particular *this*, if we are to acknowledge the validity of a more universal *that*.

Furthermore, it has been commonly accepted by Christian thinkers in every age that enough is known of God, however vaguely and imperfectly, and granted whatever error or falsehood there may be in the ways of knowing, for God to use when he evaluates each human life. No thoughtful Christian has assumed that it is *he* or *she* who 'saves' people. It is always *God* who does that. Any of us who is Christian knows full well that he or she is but the instrument through which God acts in bringing the good news of Christ to others. Thus to serve is an imperative for the devoted Christian; but it does not imply that God withholds his grace until and unless we have managed to proclaim the gospel. God is more generous than that; it is too bad if we seek to narrow his love so that it is even less generous than that of us humans with others of our kind. After all, our human imperception and arrogance are hardly an appropriate measure for God's grace. 'The love of God', says the well-known hymn, 'is broader than the measure of man's mind.' That same hymn goes on to say, 'And the heart of the Eternal is most wonderfully kind.' In other words, God's graciousness is so 'abounding', that it can bring within its range all of his children, even (and perhaps especially) those whom in our sin and self-centredness we might wish to reject or condemn.

Witnesses to God

If God has nowhere left himself 'without witness', we must enquire in just what this witness consists. The first thing to say is that it is most various. Different people, at different times, in different places, have been given this witness in a fashion which it is possible for them to discern and accept. We have already seen that in the order of nature and in human experience there is something of what we now style 'a witness to God.' In the sequence of the seasons, in the richness and beauty of nature, and in the natural provision for our needs, there is just such a witness. So also in human relationships with family and friends, in our social groupings, and in the structures of human community, there is a witness. However, we are thinking at the moment of the specifically religious ways in which human beings are given a witness to God. That suggests that we should say a little about the great non-Christian religions in all their variety and with their many different kinds of teaching.

This is no place, nor have I sufficient knowledge, to make an adequate examination of those non-Christian religious traditions. There are plenty of books which do this. But what can be done for our present purpose is to mention briefly some of the central convictions of these several religions. This is not too difficult in our own day, thanks to increasing inter-communication among the nations and the extensive travel which modern technology has made possible. Much more is known about non-Christians than was once the case. Back in the days when it took weeks or months to get to Asia, for instance, very little could be known by the ordinary person about the beliefs of Confucians, Taoists, Hindus, Sikhs, Muslims, and Buddhists in that continent. No longer is this the case. And the presence in our own land of great numbers who believe and practice another religion makes it all the easier to gain some knowledge of these non-Christian faiths.

Among the Chinese

In China for many centuries two traditions vied for acceptance. One was Taoism, associated with the name of Lao-Tsu, about whom nothing much is know and who is even thought by some scholars to be a mythological figure. The other tradition was Confucianism, which went through many transformations during the centuries but which until the Communist take-over remained the quasi-official religious world view of that country. What were the dominant aspects of these two traditions?

Taoism in its earlier form was the teaching that behind and through the whole world there is the *Tao*, an untranslatable word but usually rendered as 'the Way.' This *Tao* rejects all coercive action and does its work in the world by gentle, slow, and persistent means. Many Taoist sayings illustrate this; for example, that water, dropping quietly but ceaselessly upon a rock, can reduce that rock in size and can produce remarkable results which in the long run will be more effective than a sudden but temporary explosion of force. In the case of force the water will only run off without any lasting effect. Taoism urges that the only happiness possible for men and women is obtained when they seek to align themselves humbly and modestly with the 'way things go in the world'. Struggle against that natural order of things produces dissatisfaction and misery.

Can we not see in this religious tradition some hint that behind the visible and tangible world there is a power which works quietly and persistently? And does this not suggest that those who follow the *Tao* are in touch with what is in fact the case – namely that it is love and gentleness, rather than might and struggle, which accomplish most in the affairs of men? If I am right about this, then we can see here some intimation of the nature of God, who in the climactic Christian revelation is disclosed as nothing other than the cosmic Lover.

In Confucianism, the basic teaching is about the ordered life in which every person plays his or her part in the common existence, with reverence for those above and concern for those below. (One can hardly speak of women, in this tradition, for women seemed to have had a very inferior place and to be thought hardly worth considering!) Human society was to reflect what was believed to be the pattern manifested in the stars and other heavenly bodies as they went their way on their appointed course. Once a year the head of state – in later years the Emperor – would lead a religious ceremony in which 'the heavens' were worshipped and petition made that human affairs might be an imitation of the heavenly order. The Confucians emphasized modesty, benevolence, and duty. References to deity were few but scholars who have looked into the subject tell us that this was not intended to deny or neglect deity. Rather it reflected what Confucius is believed to have taught: he thought that humans should not enquire too closely into that which was beyond their understanding, but should behave in a truly human way, and by a modest, benevolent, and responsible life obey what he called the 'will of heaven.' Here too may we not find some dim hint or intimation of the truth that men and women are meant to seek to live in society with one another, with mutual helpfulness, with care that they do their duty where they happen to live and work, and with a becoming modesty in their claims to know 'the truth of things entire'? God was at work here.

In India and Eastern Asia

If we turn now to Hinduism, we discover that there are two main streams in that tradition. One is a highly intellectual philosophical enquiry into the basic reality behind the world of appearance. The other is the popular expression of faith in various divine beings who are worshipped by the simple sometimes with extraordinary devotion. The former type of Hinduism raised, and sought to answer, inescapable questions as to the origin of the world; the value of human experience in the world; and the way to get beyond the world's evils, which are obvious and frightening, to a reality which guarantees for human existence a significance which nothing can destroy. The end-product of this kind of Hinduism is a variety of pantheism (or better, of monism) whose defect is a too ready acceptance of this world because in the long run it is only *maya* or the 'play' of the basic divine reality (or *brahma*) which abides unchanged and eternal. Yet there is here a genuine quest for the meaning of human existence and for the realisation of a relationship with the divine reality which is behind that existence. Unhappily, that relationship seems to be interpreted as absorption in deity instead of genuine contact with a divine person who actually loves each of his creatures.

The second type of Hinduism is polytheistic. It deals with a number of divine or quasi-divine beings, whose devotee worships them and finds strength from obeying them. At its highest, in the Bhagavad-Gita, this kind of Hinduism reaches a very remarkable and moving level, as when the god Krishna discloses himself to his subject Arjuna and receives from him complete devotion and dedication. One could almost say that in relation to Krishna the follower finds a sort of 'salvation', because he is 'redeemed' from self-concern, is given a task to perform, and is assured of victory in his battle against evil in himself and in the world about him. Other gods play a similar role in other varieties of Hinduism of this type. At the back of much that is to us horrifying, as well as unpleasant, in its portrayal in myth and legend, there is a dim perception of the truth that worship is essential to human life and that obedience to the divine, however conceived, is the proper mode of human living when it is at its best.

What has been written in the last half-dozen paragraphs is very partial. Perhaps in some respects it will be criticised as not entirely accurate, for scholars and observers differ in their accounts of these religious traditions. I have tried to give a rapid survey of two or three religions that have commanded the allegiance of millions of men and women. We might have spoken about Buddhism, which again is in two forms, one the Hinayana type which to us westerners seems to be agnostic if not atheist, the other the Mahayana type in which the Buddha himself becomes the object of worship and imitation. Had we discussed Buddhism we should have been compelled to notice how its teaching, in both its forms, proclaims the need for compassion and sympathy among men and women. Its techniques of prayer or meditation, and its capacity to incorporate into itself a great number of elements that were present in the several lands to which it was carried, would have been discussed. Or we might have spoken of Islam, in which obedience to the will of Allah is the central teaching, with an almost fanatical devotion to the one who the prophet Mohammed said was not only 'all-powerful' but also 'all-compassionate.' Again, we might have spoken of the primitive religions found in 'darkest Africa', in the islands of the Pacific, in Australia, and in many other places. To us these religions often appear barbarous, superstitious, and accompanied by horrifying rites and sacrificial ceremonies. Some anthropologists, however, have urged that behind these less attractive features there is a dim belief in 'the great God' who remains hidden from men. They may be mistaken in this theory; but the fact yet remains that such primitive religions do recognise the human need to worship and manifest the belief that only by the favour of the gods who are thus worshipped can human existence be worthwhile.

Christian faith in a religious world

I am not claiming, for a moment, that these religious traditions, primitive or developed, are equal to or identical with Jewish and Christian faith. I am not advocating a syncretism in which all religions are thought to be saying the same thing in differing idiom. Obviously that is *not* the case. What I am saying is that there is a pervasive religious sense, however inadequately or mistakenly expressed, which seems to be an ineradicable part of human nature. Ultimately, in my view, this tells us that God's common grace, working through religious traditions such as we have mentioned, has been active in the affairs of his human children. He has never left himself 'without witness', even if the misunderstanding of his children has distorted that witness.

Practically speaking, this suggests that we should be ready to see that God has continually worked with his human creatures, seeking to prepare them for better things which are to come. He has used their religious sense. Indeed he has called forth or evoked that religious sense from men and women of all cultures, races, types, and nations. Building upon that but bringing to it the wonder of the gospel of God's grace in Jesus Christ our Lord, the Christian can trust that God will gladly disclose himself more fully and will act ever more intensively, until the day comes when all his children will adore him as he has now shown himself to us all in our Lord Jesus Christ.

5

'The Grace of our Lord Jesus Christ'

SUMMARY: *In the Christian response to what God has 'determined, dared, and done' in Jesus Christ, his grace is present with an intensity and speciality which both humbles us and makes us zealous in sharing this wonderful gift with other men and women. Thus we seek to bring them the richness of life-in-grace which God grants to those who are disciples of Christ.*

After what has been urged in the last two chapters, to turn as we now do to 'the grace of our Lord Jesus Christ' is for the Christian to find himself at last upon home-ground. It is that grace known to us in our experience of Christian discipleship which is most familiar to us. We live by it; we rejoice in it; we have found our wholeness of life or salvation through it. So it might well be asked: 'Why then all this earlier discussion? Is it not irrelevant to the great reality which makes us Christians 'tick?'

The answer is that the wonder of God's grace in Jesus our Lord and Saviour, the abounding love of God active towards us through him, becomes all the more wonderful when it is put in the context of that same God's never-failing action and presence in the whole creation, in every human life, and not least in the religious traditions by which those who have not met Jesus have yet found some purpose and value in life. There is no need for us to 'reduce' the speciality of God's grace in Jesus. Indeed, to do so would be disloyal to what we have gratefully received despite our unworthiness and sin. On the other hand, simply to reject out of hand those other manifestations of God's loving concern for his children would be equally disloyal – this time disloyal to the very character of God revealed to us in Jesus. For God, if he is in fact what in Jesus we know him to be, would not and could not withhold himself entirely from those of his children in all their millions who have never had the opportunity to hear about our Saviour. It would be to turn the God who in Wesley's already quoted words is 'pure unbounded love' into a monster who altogether condemned or refused millions of his children simply for their ignorance of Christ, an ignorance for which they have no responsibility. A God like that would not be 'the God and Father of our Lord Jesus Christ'; he would be a narrow-minded and arbitrary despot.

With that much understood, then, we now turn confidently to the glory of God's grace in Jesus, his redeeming, justifying, enriching, enabling, and sanctifying grace which is brought to us in the Lord whom we adore and in whose steps we seek to walk.

In the chapter following this one we shall look at those ways in which the grace of God in Jesus Christ brings us what theologians have called 'justification' – that is, how it sets us right with God, as we could never be set right by our own efforts or by anything we may try to do to 'earn salvation.' We shall consider how this means the forgiveness of which we stand in such great need since once again of ourselves and by ourselves we can never have forgiveness for our sins. We shall see how there is an enabling and a reconciliation provided by grace, which strengthen us to life 'in Christ' (as Paul puts it so many times in his letters)

42

and to be established in a relationship both with God and our fellow humans that is marked by the overcoming of alienation and of enmity. Finally, we shall speak of 'sanctification', again a theological term, which points to the wonderful reality of our becoming at one with God through Christ so that our very existence is set on the path which leads to what John Wesley called 'scriptural holiness', to the life in the Spirit released in Christ as the road to perfection which we are called to follow and for which we are 'engraced' to make that following possible for us.

Christ the giver of grace

But now we must consider what is in fact intended by that very phrase, 'the grace of our Lord Jesus Christ.' We recall our insistence in the opening pages of this book that grace is not something separate from God but is, rather, God's own working and hence his real presence. Thus we are led at once to meditate upon the person of Jesus himself, of whose 'grace' our phrase speaks.

To speak of the 'person of Christ' is essentially to speak of the historical event of which that person is the centre. This brings us to still another point to which we must give our attention. One of the misfortunes of Christian history has been the way in which of necessity the basic deliverances of biblical faith got themselves phrased in language, and with the use of ideas, drawn from Greek philosophy of a certain type which was alien to scriptural ways of thinking. I have said that this was a matter 'of necessity' and so it was, since the primitive gospel message, once it was introduced by the apostles and others into the Graeco-Roman world of the time, was naturally and inevitably brought into contact with the prevalent culture of that period. This was indeed 'necessary', because wherever Christian faith is accepted people converted to it cannot avoid bringing to their understanding of it their own ways of thinking and feeling. It is not received in a vacuum but by men and women who are what they are, think as they think, and feel as they feel. Many years may be required to correct, so far as may be, and sometimes even entirely to reject, notions that are not appropriate to the great affirmations of biblical faith.

There are two ways in which previous accepted thought affected the understanding of the gospel. The first was through the pervasive influence of the surrounding culture. A clear instance of this in the early period we are now discussing was the way in which the healthy and positive attitude to human sexuality, so markedly present in the Bible, was seriously distorted by the anti-body, anti-flesh, anti-sex attitudes that were so widespread in Hellenistic culture. The second way was much more direct and obvious. This was the almost inevitable use by Christians of ideas, notions, and intellectual concepts which were generally accepted in the world of the time. Here we have to do with philosophical views and with the idiom used to state them. Sometimes those were quite different from and contradictory to the scriptural position.

The 'model' of God

So it came about that the biblical 'model' or picture of God was modified, in fact often radically changed, when Christian thinkers began to work out their intellectual statement of what Christian faith is all about. Instead of stressing God as active, dynamic, living, and above all loving Creator, the tendency was to talk about God in terms of 'substance' – which is a 'thing' idea. Thus people began to define God in words that suggest divine inability to experience suffering as well as joy; they were led to model him after an 'unmoved mover' (to use the phrase of Aristotle) or an abstract 'primal being' (to use Platonic idiom). In doing this, they could forget (or at least seriously neglect) the biblical portrayal of God as essentially the *active* one who is pictured more after personal analogies than after 'thing' analogies.

Nowhere did this show itself so clearly as in the fashion of speaking of our Lord Jesus Christ himself. There was talk about 'two substances', one divine and the other human, somehow united in a third 'something' called 'the God-Man.' That is not biblical language. The intention of those early Christian thinkers was entirely sound. They knew that in and through Jesus they had been met by God himself; they knew that Jesus had lived as a man among men; and they knew that this Jesus, in whom God was active in human existence, was *one* person, not a divided or split being. That is what they wanted to express. But unhappily, their choice of language, inevitable at the time, led to grave misunderstanding and in many ways has had unhappy consequences. To recognise this is not in any way to attack the great thinkers who were responsible; they were doing the best they could if they were to use the language and ideas of Hellenistic culture. At the same time, we have no need to 'canonize' their language, as if it were directly inspired by God and had been validated by him as true for all times and in all places.

Thinking of God dynamically

One result of this fashion of thinking has been the very odd and entirely unscriptural separation of God's 'presence' and God's 'activity' to which I referred in the opening chapter. With respect to the 'person of Christ', this has meant an even more odd and much more unscriptural separation of our Lord and Saviour as a 'person' from our Lord and Saviour as the human, yet divinely prepared and divinely empowered, activity of God. In a wider sense, we can see in much western thinking, even up to our own day, a readiness to talk of the creation and of ourselves entirely in 'thing' terms. But biblical talk (and also, as an important fact in our own day, the talk of modern scientists too) is always in 'event' idiom. Robert Louis Stevenson's well-known children's verse, which says that 'the world is so full of a number of *things*', is wrong. However convenient such an expression may be, the truth is that the world is *not* made up of things but of *happenings*. It is a world of events, not one of 'substances' or 'self-subsistent' entities.

I must apologize for what may seem a somewhat abstract technical discussion during the last few paragraphs. But as a matter of fact what has just been said is not at all abstract and not particularly technical. It is simply common sense. We all know what is being urged here. Its relevance to 'the grace of our Lord Jesus Christ' is, or ought to be, apparent at a glance. For if God's grace is God himself in loving activity in the world, and if God is no *thing* separable from what that 'thing' does but rather is himself loving divine Activity (I capitalise to make plain that here we are speaking of the supremely worshipful, dependable, and unsurpassable deity), then certainly to say 'the grace of our Lord Jesus Christ' is to say something which is of enormous importance. It is to say that Jesus Christ is that particular instance of human existence, that person in his own time and place, in whom 'very God of very God' is active in true manhood – and he is active there for what the ancient Nicene Creed styles 'us men and our salvation.' In other words, the grace *of Jesus Christ* our Lord is *God's* working in and through him, so that he is indeed 'very God in very man', one with the Father who sent him and one with us to whom he was sent. This is the indisputable claim of Christian faith, with its source in the New Testament and its verification in the experience of newness of life, forgiveness of sin, fellowship with God, and redemptive love which each of us, as a Christian, can humbly declare to be the gift which through Christ we have received.

46

God has acted in love

We recall once more the great words of John in his First
Letter which tell us that 'God is love.' We recall also that
in the very same portion of that letter in which those words
occur, we are told that this wonderful truth is made known
to us because 'God loved us and sent his Son, that we
might live through him.' This is indeed God's amazing
grace declared to us in something which God had done.
The English poet Christopher Smart spoke of what God
had 'determined, dared, and done in Jesus.' Is that
exaggeration? I believe not. For it is an assertion that God
has taken risks in acting in Jesus to accomplish through
him the salvation of the children of his love. God has
determined to do this, out of his enormous concern for his
erring children; he has *dared* to do this, knowing full well
the danger of contemptuous rejection and the likelihood
of what indeed did take place – betrayal and crucifixion;
and he has *done* this, by acting in the total event of Jesus
Christ so that the world thereafter has become a different
place, different because (from then on) God and humanity
were brought together in a definitive and special manner.

I wish to argue, therefore, that we must not use the
words which are the title of this chapter in an easy and
indifferent fashion.

A new vision of God in Christ

Those words open up to us a vision of God which can be
expressed in no other way. They link together God's grace
and our Lord Jesus Christ, in a union which is an abiding
reality and is no mere incident nor accident which might
make little if any impact upon us. This is why the
Christian ages have been impatient of any minimising of
the divinity *or* of the humanity found in Jesus. What in
theology is called Christ's 'benefits' are the amazingly

good things which have been given to us in and through him: 'the redemption of the world by our Lord Jesus Christ, the means of grace, and the hope of glory', to repeat again the phrases from the old General Thanksgiving prayer.

On the one hand, in Christian history there have been those who think that we should so stress the divine act in Jesus Christ that we tend to minimise the wonder of the human life in Palestine. This is the 'heresy' – the very partial and hence erroneous view – that for some reason often seems attractive to those who pride themselves on being highly 'orthodox.' An acquaintance of mine was once talking in this way, saying that he believed that Jesus was so divine that his humanity was really almost irrelevant in his own Christian discipleship. I replied that in that case, his view had 'been condemned as heresy by the Church as far back as 381 A.D., at the First Council of Constantinople, under the name of "Apollinarianism."' Of course I was showing off in a naughty way my theological awareness.

But perhaps my response was a useful reminder to my friend that the Christian Church has always insisted on the genuine and full manhood of its Lord. It has never accepted the position so jauntily and inaccurately stated by one of my students, many years ago, 'I think that Jesus is God with a skin on.' No; the Church knows that the grace of God in our Lord Jesus Christ is indeed as divine as divinity can be, but also knows that it is made available to us through a genuine human agency.

But on the other hand, there have been those who have tended to think of Jesus as an exceptionally good man, a divinely-inspired man if you will, but not to go beyond this. This 'heresy' has its particular attraction, it would seem, for those who pride themselves on being peculiarly 'up to date' and for those who take altogether too exalted a view of human existence and its capability. Once again, the Christian centuries have never been able to adopt any such 'reductionist' position about their Lord. That he was indeed genuinely and truly human they have believed and taught. Yet they have gone on to say, with the sure conviction of faith, that they have been met in him by God, in a fashion which makes understandable the old language about his being 'God-Man' – even if that particular way of expressing it may not appeal to us today, with its implicit background in talk of two 'substances' or things (one divine, the other human) somehow made one in him. The point is that only *God*, God's own grace which is God himself in loving action, could redeem us. The Christian ages have known this very well indeed.

Thus talk of 'the grace of our Lord Jesus Christ' is talk about God in action there and then, in that man, at that time, and in that place. We must not whittle down this bold affirmation. Furthermore, as we have urged, we must not separate God and God's grace with the result that we make the latter only a secondary affair. To do that would be to miss part of the glory and wonder of the love of God, which is God's 'very essence' active towards us – and supremely in the Lord and Saviour whom we adore and seek to follow.

In our human experience

We have tried in each chapter of this book to stress the practical implications which follow from what has been urged about grace. Perhaps some may think that there is little need to reiterate the practical implications of the abounding grace of God in that one in whom, as a New Testament text says, 'God's grace has appeared to us.' Yet something must be said.

For instance, we may follow the thought suggested in some of the writings of the great Danish thinker of the last century Søren Kierkegaard. He spoke of Jesus as the pattern of human living for each one of us who is called to do what he styled 'the works of love' in following the

Master. But Kierkegaard went on to say that in the case of Jesus, unlike that of Socrates with whom he made a comparison, the pattern has become a *power* – the New Testament, we may remember, speaks about 'the power of endless life' made available in Jesus. Those two words, power and pattern, can give us practical guidance in our discipleship. For they tell us that we are able only to 'imitate' our Lord Jesus Christ when we are open to the empowering which he provides for his faithful. The pattern will then refer to 'following the blessed steps of his most holy life', as an old prayer puts it; and the power will refer to the strength, which God alone can give, to make such a following possible for us. Thus Jesus is our comrade and brother, whose human life was marked by filial obedience to the heavenly Father and a zealous concern to do what God purposed for him to do. He is also our Lord, our Saviour, whom we adore and in whom we find 'more than we can desire or think' for our effort in seeking to manifest in our own place and way that same filial obedience and jealous concern.

Furthermore, the word grace includes, as has frequently been pointed out in these pages and elsewhere, two conceptions or notions. One is the divine favour or loving interest in God's human children; the other is the divine energy or activity released into the world as God moves towards it and works in it. Thus in a very practical way we have the assurance that despite our sin, our defects, our foolishness, and all the other things that mar our lives, God still and always loves us and is concerned for us. In Pauline language, while 'we were yet sinners' God loved us and was prepared to accept us. Now that we are *forgiven* sinners, he still loves us and is concerned for us. We can count on God always to do for us that which we of ourselves could never do. God will act favourably towards us, for us, and in us. He will never desert us. He will keep us close to himself – and all that *we* need do is simply to trust him and commit ourselves to him. 'His grace is sufficient for me.'

Finally, confidence in 'the grace of our Lord Jesus Christ' delivers us from what a prayer calls 'faithless fears and worldly anxieties.' It emboldens us to live bravely and joyously as his children. It frees us from fear, above all from the fear of death – both our own death and the death of those who are dear to us. In our seventh chapter we shall speak about this at some length, seeing in it what we shall call 'the fulfilment of grace.' Here and now, however, we can say that such deliverance from fears and anxieties of all kinds, and above all from dread about the fact that all of us must die, is one of our greatest human needs.

Christ frees us from fear

In the familiar song from 'Showboat', the musical play of a couple of generations ago, one of the characters says of 'Ole Man River' that it 'just keeps rolling along.' And then he says of himself, 'I'm tired of living and scared of dying.' Are there not times when each of us feels that way? Perhaps in the long hours of the night when we cannot get to sleep, we may have the sense of 'quiet desperation' of which Henry Thoreau once wrote as being universal among men and women. There are moments when our existence seems inane and pointless, without worth or value. There are those other moments when the thought of death, whether it is a near reality or a more remote one, frightens us. Above all, there are those moments when we have lost somebody dear to us, somebody 'whom we have loved long since and lost awhile'. We are in anguish about this breaking of a relationship which has made our life significant and beautiful. In all those moments, as also in the ordinary daily anxieties and worries which nobody can escape, God's grace in Jesus Christ assures us that there *is* meaning and value, that we have *not* been bereft of all

51

companionship and comfort, and that we *are* loved and cared for by the Father of us all.

When we go through the bad spots, those dark valleys in which there seems no light and no help, we can remember that 'Christ leads us through no darker rooms than he went through before.' For 'the grace of our Lord Jesus Christ' was not enacted in the bright and happy hours only; it knew darkness and despair ('My God, my God, why hast thou forsaken me?' Jesus cried from the Cross), quite as much as joy and gladness. Thus from a steadying contemplation of God's grace in our Lord Jesus Christ we can come to see that even if we 'go down to hell, *he* is there also.' We can know that when our 'heart and strength fails' God is still 'our portion for ever' and that his 'right hand upholds us.' I have been quoting here from different places in Scripture, Old and New Testament. They indicate the practical side of our faith that in our Lord Jesus Christ the grace of God has appeared among us. They lead us to commit ourselves, all that we have and all whom we love, to that same grace which will never fail us, never let us down.

Now and again when I think of these things I am most certainly amazed. I am confirmed in my faith that if in Jesus 'God be for us, who can be against us', and strengthened in my conviction that it is true – in the most profound sense of that word – that 'nothing can separate us from the love of God which is in Christ Jesus our Lord.' Could anything be more practical, in our daily living, than that assurance?

6

Life in Grace:

Forgiveness, Justification, Reconciliation, Enabling, Sanctification

SUMMARY: *Our life in grace assures us of God's forgiveness, our being 'set right with him', our experiencing reconciliation or at-one-ment with him and with our human brothers and sisters, our receiving strength to persevere in Christian living, and our 'sanctification', so that we become people more worthy of God's care. The Christian sacraments, especially Holy Communion, are crucial means by which this grace is made available to us.*

In beginning the preceding chapter I promised that in the following one I would write about the ways in which Christ's 'benefits' – the consequences of 'the grace of our Lord Jesus Christ' – are worked out in the lives of those who respond to him in commitment and trust.

I suggested that these might be considered under five heads: forgiveness, justification, reconciliation, enabling, and sanctification. I must now redeem that promise and invite the reader's attention to these five, always remembering that in the end of the day we are concerned not so much with the theological niceties that are involved – although these are important and I should be the last person to minimise them – but with the practical implications which they have for our Christian attitudes and actions.

We must begin by making clear once more that the Christian life is made possible through God's abounding grace, not by our own efforts or achievements. Grace is *given* to us; it is a gift which we cannot earn by anything that we say or think or do. It is *gratuitous*, as the saying goes; that is to say that it is given to us without prior conditions and is to be gratefully accepted for what it is. In this way, grace is like love; indeed, I have already urged that grace *is* God's love in action and hence God himself *in* action. Nobody would ever claim, if he or she had experience of life, that one can earn or merit love on the part of another person. It is always a gift, something we know ourselves to be unworthy to receive and something which no amount of effort on our own part could win.

Grace is always gift

It is true, of course, that one who would be loved must also be one who loves and hence one who can recognise and appreciate love when it comes. But the young man who finds himself truly loved by another person would not for a moment assert that he had deserved or earned what he was receiving from that other. The girl who loves him does this, not because he has somehow or other done the right things, like showering her with presents, taking her to dances, flattering her in an effort to please. He may indeed do all those things and yet find that the girl does not love him at all. She may even think his attentions odious and may the more readily come to dislike him. The truth is that in such deep relationships, the presents and the other attentions paid by the young man are basically his way of saying 'Thank you' and thereby expressing his gratitude

54

for the 'amazing love' which she feels for him and shows towards him.

The point here, in respect to the relationship between God our loving heavenly Parent and ourselves as his unworthy children, is not that we are to do nothing, but rather that what we do is a response. As Martin Luther used to urge, good works on our part are not the *condition* of our being redeemed by God in Christ; they are the *consequence* of our being redeemed. They are pleasing to God because they are sincere expressions of our thankfulness to him for his having taken us to himself by his gracious acceptance long before we made any return of any sort to him.

I have laboured this point because many of us, perhaps more especially Anglo-Saxon people, seem to have a tendency to be what religious thinkers call 'Pelagian' in our attitude. That is, we resemble those who in the earlier days of the Church made altogether too pretentious claims about their achievements and who had to be shown (by St Augustine and others) to be mistaken in their assumption that of themselves they could win God's approval. It is true that now and again people have pushed this Augustinian emphasis to an extreme; they have spoken of human existence as a vile and utterly corrupt thing. They have seemed sometimes to turn the good news of God's free grace in Jesus Christ into the bad news (however partially true) that we are *only* sinners. We most certainly are sinners, and grievous ones at that; yet we must not denigrate God's creation nor consider ourselves to be only and solely evil people. On the other hand, we must recognize the patent fact that the more we try to earn merit in God's sight the more we fall into self-centredness and become graceless and unhappy. Perhaps here I should not have said 'graceless', since no human being is ever without something of God's grace working in him or her. Upon that truth we have already spoken in earlier discussion of basic Christian conviction. Yet the word 'graceless' *can* serve, in the sense that to count too much on self and self's achievements is a denial of the need for grace and a refusal to put God's grace in the central place which belongs to him and to him alone. We then can become even more horribly 'twisted in upon ourselves', as Luther put it in his famous Latin phrase that each of us is *incurvatus in se*. Translation is easy to make. In a way our human condition is precisely that twisting in upon ourselves, thinking of ourselves as 'monarchs of all we survey', relying on ourselves and feeling proud of what we do. There is no need to aggravate that condition by *false* pride, as modern 'Pelagians', like their ancestors, are prone to do. Humility about ourselves and readiness to see our human insufficiency are much more seemly and becoming, as they are much closer to the facts of the case.

Our gift of self to God

But here a proviso is required. I have just been saying that no man, no woman, is able to win or earn salvation or a right relationship with God. I have *not* been saying that we are unable to contribute anything to God; I have *not* been saying that human existence is a worthless affair; and I have *not* been saying that God is uninfluenced by, unconcerned about, and unable or unwilling to receive from his creatures anything at all. On the contrary, I believe that God does care for us and our response, that he is receptive of that which his creation can achieve, and that he is influenced or affected by what goes on in that creation. Perhaps this requires a word of explanation.

We have seen that the importation of Hellenistic notions into Christian thought had unhappy consequences so far as the 'doctrine of the person of Christ' is concerned. Now we must go on to say that this importation had equally unhappy consequences in respect to our picture of God in his relationship with the creation. Because those Hellenistic ideas viewed God as remote from the world, they also implied that he is unaffected by what goes on in that world. But the Bible does not talk like that. In Scripture God is most intimately concerned with his world and is very profoundly affected by what goes on there. It can bring him joy; it can cause anguish to his loving heart. He adapts himself with great wisdom and discernment to the creation. Hence he must – and his nature is such that he can – adjust his activity to those creaturely situations and circumstances, taking account of and using the events in the world so that the best may be accomplished and his over-arching purpose may be fulfilled. Furthermore it may be noted that nowhere in the Bible is there talk about God as he is 'in himself', so to say; everything said about God, from the first creation stories in Genesis straight through to the portrayal of the final consummation in the Book of Revelation, is said about him in relationship with the world, of which he is creator, sustainer, and loving yet sovereign Lord.

In respect to redemption our human impotence is to be asserted, but not to insist on excluding all possible contributions which the created order may make to the furthering of the divine will or to the impeding of that will. It is essential that this distinction be carefully made and its implications followed. Unless we do this we shall end up with a view of God which is other than biblical and perhaps even radically *un*biblical. We shall denigrate God's creation with the result that it becomes an inane and meaningless enterprise.

We turn now to look at the grace of God, active in Jesus Christ, as the means for the forgiveness of our sin, the justification or setting-right of men and women with God, their reconciliation with God and hence with one another, their receiving strength or enablement to live in accordance with the divine purpose, and their growth in holiness or sanctification as they are opened to God's gracious working in them. We shall consider each of these in turn.

Forgiveness

Forgiveness, like justification with which it is closely associated, is not so much retrospective as prospective. Obviously it includes readiness to pardon past offences, but its primary direction is towards the future. To be forgiven – even at the human level, as when a friend forgives me for the wrong that I have done him or her – is to be given the assurance that what has happened in the past will not impede our future relationship one with the other. To be forgiven is to be accepted and cared for, in spite of what may have taken place. When you forgive me, you are in effect saying that you still care for me and that you will treat me as your friend. Furthermore, this is something that we cannot do of ourselves and for ourselves. All of us know that people sometimes say, 'I couldn't forgive myself' for doing this or that. That is always profoundly true. Nobody can forgive himself or herself. Forgiveness must be granted us, given us, provided for us, by the ones we have offended.

How do we offend God? Or in other words, what is *sin*? A good deal of supposedly Christian teaching on this subject seems to suggest that sin is a matter merely of violating laws or breaking rules: But the Bible is quite clear that sin is much more serious than that.

For the Bible, sin is the breaking or violation of a *relationship*. We are made in God's image and are meant to reflect his likeness. This carries with it the corollary that sin is a refusal of God's image, although that image can never be completely destroyed since it is *God's* image in us. Sin is also a negation of God's likeness in us. The way in which this occurs is by our deciding to live on our own, to neglect God, in fact to want to break down the relationship of love on his part towards us. Love still continues, of course, despite all that we may do. Yet to refuse, *on our part*, filial obedience and loyal commitment to him and his will does take place. The particular *sins* (in

58

the plunal) of which we are guilty are the expression of that relationship which has been broken by us. When we no longer live in the relationship of a son or daughter to our heavenly Parent we do what is bad for us and hurtful to him. The commandments are guidelines given by God to help us live in the right relationship with him. The breaking of them is a manifestation of the dreadful fact that we do not really want to live in that relationship and prefer to go our own way, regardless of him and regardless also of the human possibilities which he has established for us to enjoy.

But God still loves us. 'While we were yet sinners', at enmity with God, he took action on our behalf. This is a central part of the gospel; it assures us that 'Christ died for us' – to continue the text just cited – so that we might be brought back into the right relationship with our God. Henceforth, once we have been ready to accept what has been done on our behalf, we are treated by God as if we were indeed what, at the moment, alas! we are not: as his loyal and devoted sons and daughters. This is what forgiveness is all about.

Justification

The Greek word *dikaiosune* which is behind the English term 'Justification' can be translated in various ways. That is why different Christian thinkers have drawn out in different ways what is implied in that word. It can mean 'setting right', 'making right', or 'being accepted as right.' Probably it means *all* of these at one and the same moment. What it is asserting is that through something that God has done sinful men and women, who are in a wrong relationship with God, are through that divine act put into a right relationship, accounted for or accepted as being in that relationship. And this is through no effort of their own, but because of God's never-failing grace towards them.

The well-known thinker Paul Tillich, who died only a few years ago, made a useful suggestion about this. He urged that what is at stake here is what he called our 'acceptance.' As things stand, we are not acceptable to God since we have rejected our inheritance as his sons and daughters and sought to live in our own way. But, he said, the 'new being in Christ' (as he called the total event denoted by the name of our Saviour) is such that we can now know that we *have been accepted*, despite our utter unacceptability. If we will by faith accept our being accepted, he urged, we are released from bondage to the old self in its alienation and estrangement from God. We are set free to live in 'newness of life' and incorporated into 'new being in Christ', so that he may live in us and we in him. And we may be adopted into his own wonderful sonship to God. As the old Church writers, centuries ago, liked to put it, we are made 'sons in *the* Son' (*filii in Filio*).

When we know that we are accepted by God – accounted righteous in his sight and enabled to live in terms of that acceptance – we are able then to accept both ourselves and other people. We need no longer be afraid of ourselves but only aware of our human feebleness and hence of our constant need for God's help. Nor need we fear other people and what they may do to us, for they too are in God's loving hands and can be brought to seek peace, concord, and understanding. What is more, we can 'cast our burdens on the Lord'; we know now that he will always accept us and what we try to do. And he will make of us and of our actions the best that can possibly be made.

Reconciliation

Forgiven by God and set right with him, we experience reconciliation, first and most important with God and then as a consequence with our fellow men and women. And reconciliation is something we need desperately.

We look at the world around us, with its racial antagonisms, its power struggles, its absence of understanding between people, its increasing rate of divorce, its violence and war. Among us humans there is antagonism, hatred, jealousy, and horrible fear. All of us know this to be true. What we do not seem to see is that behind this situation there is another alienation and estrangement – between God and his human children. As St Paul says, we are at enmity with our Creator, despite all that he has done and is doing for us. We need reconciliation all along the line, first with God and then with our fellows. It is the Christian proclamation that in Christ God 'has reconciled us to himself'; and in response we are to be 'ministers of reconciliation.' By God's grace, released for us in Christ, we are to labour for the overcoming of dissension among nations, between the sexes, in racial relationships, and in every other area, including industrial unrest and distrust and all that follows from these.

It would be naive to think that with the establishment of reconciliation between God and his children all our problems will be done away. On the contrary, it might be argued that when we know God's grace in Jesus Christ and have experienced reconciliation with him, our human problems may seem worse than they were before. Why is this? I think the answer is that through divine-human reconciliation we are made keenly aware of the *heights* of human possibility, which we so tragically fail to achieve or even to seek, while at the same time we become keenly aware of the *depths* to which men and women may sink, in their self-centredness, pride, arrogance, and pretension to independence. On the other hand, while reconciliation with God will not of itself solve our problems, it will give us the clue to their only possible solution – which is by shared life, with love as the motive for action and justice as the result of that action.

Faith is no cure-all

Religious faith, as our response to God's grace in Christ, is not a universal panacea; if we think it is, we shall be sadly disappointed. Further, it has often and correctly been pointed out that one of the purposes of God's coming to us in atoning love is *not* to make it unnecessary to keep our eyes open, use our heads, and strive to grasp and master situations. God has too much respect for his children to treat them as if they were puppets who are to be moved around without their own consent. He wants us to be truly human, which means responsible, free, and intelligent agents who seek to do his will, not because they are coerced into doing it but because they have been won to do it through the lure of his love coming towards them.

This is why some old-fashioned evangelists were talking nonsense, although with the best of motives, when they said that if only everybody were converted to Christ there would be no more wrong-doing in the world and an almost utopian perfection would be established among us. They were quite as mistaken as are the humanists who talk about our 'building heaven on earth' or the misguided Christian liberals of an earlier generation who urged that we should all work to 'bring in God's kingdom.' God's kingdom or sovereign rule is *God's*, not ours. It is he who will bring it in, when it comes, not we humans by our own efforts however well-intentioned and zealous. Certainly only a very unrealistic person could talk nowadays about some humanistic perfection which men and women can establish by their own efforts. As for the old-fashioned evangelists, *their* failure was that they did not take sufficiently seriously the way in which millenia of wrong choices, wrong actions, and wrong willing have brought about a situation in this world which individual human conversions, important and necessary as they are, cannot entirely and instantly change for the better. They *talked* about sin a great deal. Yet they did not recognise its wide ramifications, its permeation of human institutions and groups, and its horrifying results in what older theologians rightly saw to be the persistence of 'concupiscence' (as they called it) even among the redeemed; and by concupiscence those older theologians were pointing to the terrible way in which what the New Testament styles 'the old Adam' still continues to influence and distort our lives.

Lives Open to God

The right attitude for us who have known God's saving grace in Jesus Christ is to open ourselves continually in prayer and dedication to the operation of that grace, so that we may be 'instruments of God's peace.' That phrase is from the wonderful medieval saint, Francis of Assisi, who at the end of his life wrote or dictated a prayer in which he asked that he and his followers might thus serve God, returning good for evil, love for hatred, and help – doubtless in small ways and with little public recognition – to bring light where there was darkness, truth where there was error and falsehood, love where there was antipathy and contempt.

Beyond that personal commitment to the ways of God, you and I also have a Christian obligation to align ourselves with causes, movements, agencies, organisations, and campaigns which are working for reconciliation among men and nations. I shall not pursue this matter here, save for suggesting that one good test of our *genuine* commitment, rather than a merely verbal one, to God's purpose of love in the world is to ask ourselves and try honestly to answer such questions as these: In my own community, am *I* doing anything to develop greater understanding between races and social groups? In my business or school or shop, am *I* seeking always to promote that same sort of greater understanding? Do *I* take my part in such societies or agencies as are concerned to bring about a better world, with more justice for more people at more places and in more ways? Do *I* think of reconciliation in terms wider and more inclusive than my own position and place, my own assurance of salvation, and my own satisfaction with Sunday worship without much attention to 'Monday work'? Those are very searching questions; and I speak for myself when I must confess that I have failed and continue to fail in all these respects. Perhaps the reader will honestly admit that the same is true of him or her. We must see that like forgiveness and justification, reconciliation has very practical implications which no professing Christian can dare to evade or avoid.

Enabling

God's grace is an active, not a merely verbal or passive, affair. It is *at work* in the world. It is at work always and everywhere, as we have seen; it is at work in all human experience and in the pervasive religious sensibility natural to us all; it is at work supremely and specifically in our Lord Jesus Christ. God's grace is not something only to be talked about, although since we are talking creatures we must do just that. Above all, it is something that God does and something that demands from us a response in active service. I have already quoted Emil Brunner's golden saying, 'God's grace is our task.' That is profoundly true. It is equally true, however, that *we* are not 'sufficient for these things.' And God's grace comes in as an enabling, empowering, strengthening, and invigorating energy.

We men and women often enough have very good intentions, but we lack the will to carry them out. We know our duty in this or that situation; but where is the strength to enable us to do what we ought to do? In our weakness we fail time and time again. So we are in need of some energising force which will come to our aid. We are like a person who has been ill and discovers that she cannot do what she wishes to do, intends to do, plans to do, knows she ought to do. A tonic is required for somebody like that. Therefore she turns to her physician or goes to the chemists' shop, as we say in Britain – to the pharmacy or drug-store, in American usage. From the physician or from the pharmacist the necessary tonic is obtained. It is like that with us in our Christian living. We frequently see the necessity for vigorous activity in real discipleship. But how *can* we do what we see is the task before us? Only by the grace of God, the abounding grace which is like a tonic, which gives vitality and strength, can we move forward in our Christian vocation.

God's grace is always available to us if only we will turn to him. It is indeed already with us but we must open ourselves to its energising power and let it work through us. In our prayers we are able to open ourselves in just that fashion. Sometimes it is good for us in our times of prayer to forget our own petitions or intercessions and simply allow ourselves to bask in God's sunshine, to permit his strength to enter into us, to invigorate us, to stimulate us, to strengthen and empower us. Then perhaps some day we may be able to say with the apostle that while we ourselves have been weak, it has not been ourselves but 'the grace of God working in [us]' which has made us more genuine disciples of Christ, so that others who have observed our loyal and dedicated lives will be able to say that they 'took notice of [us] that [we] have been with Jesus.' It was *his* grace which made it possible for us to do God's will. As St Paul said, 'I can do all things through him that strengtheneth me.'

Sanctification

Some Christian teaching has made much too great a separation between justification, our being set right with

65

God, and sanctification, our growing in the holiness that comes from living closely with him. The truth is that these are two stages or moments along the Christian way, the former signifying our being put upon the right path and the latter our being enabled to walk along that path. We are 'going on to perfection', although we have not yet arrived there.

The word 'holy' is used in the Bible to describe that which, or those who, *belong to God*. In Scripture it does not have the more modern meaning of virtuous or morally good – although to belong to God naturally *includes* such a reflection of his goodness that the right moral quality follows from it. Also in the New Testament the word 'saint' does not refer to particular men and women who have been 'canonised' or recognised by some ecclesiastical council or by common consent as being numbered among the heroes and heroines of the faith. Rather, it is a word which for the writers of the New Testament simply indicates that those who have responded in faith to Jesus Christ are, and have been, brought into such a close contact with him that his own 'belonging to God' is enlarged to include them as well. You and I are 'called to be saints', first as our vocation, to the acceptance of which we are invited, and then as our continuing in that vocation in which we 'daily endeavour ourselves to follow the blessed steps of his most holy life.' The words just quoted come from one of the most beautiful prayers in the Book of Common Prayer. They are immediately preceded by other words which speak of our gratefully receiving what the prayer calls Christ's 'inestimable benefit', his working in us through grace and his conveying to us the favour and strengthening energy which God provides. To walk in Jesus' steps, with his continuing help supporting us, is the way of our sanctification.

The great English preacher and teacher John Wesley wrote a famous essay on 'Perfection,' in which he made the claim that perfection is a possibility for anybody, even in this present life. For this claim he was vigorously attacked by many critics. But I believe that their attack was based upon a misunderstanding of what Wesley was getting at; sometimes, as it seems to me, they did not really read carefully his essay on the subject. If by perfection he meant final arrival at such a state, as if it were once and for all, then doubtless he would have been wrong. But the truth is that Wesley's thought depended upon his accepting William Law's teaching that the Christian life is what Law styled 'the process of Christ' in the believer.

The point of that famous Wesley essay is essentially that once someone is on the Christian path, dependent upon God, open to divine influence, and reliant upon divine grace, he or she is *already* walking on the road which in itself is human finite perfection. To play with words, such an one may not be 'perfectly perfect'; but he or she has got the root of the matter inside, and one day – who can tell when or how? – will indeed arrive at the goal, which is loving reception by God into his own life.

Grace through sacrament

So much, then, for our consideration of forgiveness, justification, reconciliation, enabling, and sanctification. Now we must consider another point before we conclude this chapter. This has to do with what are usually called 'the means of grace.' In Christian idiom, this phrase has a wider reference but also a narrower and particular reference to worship and prayer, to baptism and confirmation, and above all to the sacramental presence and action of God in Christ known and received through the Holy Communion, the Lord's Supper, the Eucharist, the mass, or whatever other name we may wish to give the central rite in the Christian tradition of worship.

A few words about this sacrament, therefore, will be of

practical importance as we consider how God's grace is given to us.

Eucharist

There are several headings under which this sacrament may be understood: memorial or remembrance, incorporation into Christ, the 'sacrifice of praise and thanksgiving,' and the presentness of Christ to the communicant at the Lord's Table. Something should be said about each of these.

The Lord's Supper is 'the continual remembrance of the sacrifice of the death of Christ'. It has its focus in a repetition of the giving of bread and the taking of wine at the Last Supper in the Upper Room on the night before Jesus was betrayed. But since the event of Christ is a seamless whole, the sacrament also includes the remembrance of his entire life, his suffering, his surrender of himself to the Father, and his glorious resurrection from the dead.

As a 'memorial' it is not a mental turning back on our part to an historical occurrence long ago. On the contrary, it is like the Jewish Passover, in which by things done at a 'memorial meal' the past became, and for modern Jews still is, present in the experience of the chosen people. At the Lord's Supper Christ's total act becomes present with his faithful people, as they receive with thanksgiving the bread and wine which he has ordained to be eaten and drunk. It is the incorporation of these faithful people into the ongoing life of the Lord himself, so that they live in him and he lives in them.

Through this sacramental rite each of us is re-constituted as a member of the Body of Christ which is 'the blessed company of all faithful people'. We become his instruments in the world and we are renewed in dedication to his service. Thus we go out from the Holy Communion as agents whose task is to bring reconciliation to others.

Perhaps of all the aspects of God's gracious activity in the world, this is the most amazing: that through participation in the broken bread and the shared wine we are so made one with Christ that we are reconciled to God our Father and are enabled to be agents of reconciliation for our human brothers and sisters.

In recent years, Christians of the Reformation Churches have been rediscovering both the centrality and the supreme importance of the sacrament of Holy Communion. For many centuries, these Churches put very little practical stress upon the sacrament, tending rather to make the sermon the focus of worship. They forgot, for reasons that are historically understandable, that both Martin Luther and John Calvin intended the congregations which adopted their rediscovery of the gospel message in its integrity and purity, to gather each Lord's Day for an act of worship which was to include both the 'proclamation of the Word' in sermon and the 'reception of the sacrament' as a 'visible enactment' of that word. As Luther put it, 'The Word is preached in the sermon and received in the sacrament.' In many parishes and congregations in these Reformation Churches, the sacrament is celebrated with increasing frequency, sometimes every Sunday. And in the Anglican Communion this emphasis is more and more given expression – as at the Parish Communion each Sunday.

What is so interesting is that the Catholic Churches – which had always placed such emphasis on the sacrament – have found that the sermon must also have its central place. In the post-Vatican II Roman Catholic Church a sermon or 'homily' is required at every Mass attended by a congregation of any size. The Churches which spring from the Reformation are finding on their part that the sacrament must have *its* central place along with the sermon which hitherto had been given the only significant place. This remarkable meeting of two Christian traditions is highly encouraging and promises much for the future growing-together of all Christian groups.

We end this chapter, then, by noting that one of the very practical matters here involved is a more frequent, more devout, and more regular sacramental life. The reader should ask whether he or she has been caught up in this new, but yet very old, understanding that supreme among the 'means of grace', by which God in Christ is actively engaged in our human living, is the Holy Communion; and whether he or she finds joy and help in the regular and thankful reception of that sacrament in which our Lord both discloses himself to his people and 'engraces' them with singular fulness and intensity.

7

The Fulfilment of Grace

SUMMARY: *God's grace will find its fulfilment as his children are brought to abide in him forever. Here and now this is only partial because we are finite and defective creatures. In what we call 'heaven' it is brought to completion, as God receives us into his own life and employs us for his own purpose in the creation. Unfailingly he remembers us, cares for us, and uses us, for our great good and for his greater glory.*

We turn finally to a consideration of the fulfilment of God's grace, known in the world generally, at work in human experience, seen in religious sensibility, and given supremely in the 'grace of our Lord Jesus Christ.' That fulfilment may be stated quite simply. It is the gathering of all things into the everlasting life of God himself, so that in the end *nothing* is lost – nothing, that is, except evil, wickedness, and sin which as such cannot be received into God's life since he is 'of purer eyes than to behold iniquity.'

Christian life is no 'success-story'

Before we proceed with our discussion, however, there is an important prior point which must be grasped. When we speak, as in our Christian hymns and prayers we do

71

speak, of God's crowning his human endeavour and bringing all things to a good conclusion, never letting down his creation, never deserting it, never neglecting it, we are not saying that worldly success, material gain, human prosperity and the like are guaranteed to us and can be expected to be given us, simply because God loves and cares for us and for the world in which we have our dwelling. There is a tragic distortion of the Christian gospel sometimes found even in preachers and teachers who ought to know better. That distortion is expressed in the idea that if we are faithful to God, seek to do his will and live in genuine relationship with him, we are bound to be 'successful' people. We are sure to 'win friends and influence people', to have economic security and even financial gain, and in every way to be prosperous as the world judges prosperity. It is inconceivable, to my mind, that any professing Christian could think in this way. Why? Simply because at the heart of our faith is a story which whatever else it may be is most certainly *not* a human 'success story.' Our Lord and Saviour died upon the Cross. In worldly terms he was a failure, not a success. Only the eye of faith can see that divinely speaking that failure was the greatest conceivable success – which is to say that the Resurrection is a triumphant affirmation that in the anguish, suffering, and death of Jesus there is a disclosure of God as suffering love, love which *in its very suffering* secures the only significant triumph. Such love 'cannot be holden of death' nor can it fail finally to achieve its purpose for our salvation.

Has our existence any value?

The crux of the matter is this: has human existence any enduring value? That same question may be asked about the world as a whole: has that creation, so painstakingly brought into existence and so carefully sustained by God, any real significance, in the long run and with due regard for all its imperfection and the evil that is certainly present in it? If the world and human existence have no value and no significance, if they represent (in Shakespeare's famous words) only 'a tale told by an idiot, full of sound and fury, signifying nothing', then God's grace would be shown to have been ineffectual. Far from its being the sovereign fact in creation it would be only an illusion or at best a temporary activity. The indefatigable and indefeasible working of God, in his loving care and concern (which is what grace really means, as we have said over and over again), would be incompetent to do what it sets out to do, impotent in the face of obstacles, and therefore hardly a trustworthy reality upon which we may always count and to which we may appropriately be committed.

But it is the Christian claim that despite all that may appear to be contrary to God's purposes and despite the evil which is so inescapably present in the world, grace *is* to be trusted: it *is* to be counted upon; it *never* lets us down. I have said 'despite' what seems to negate and deny grace, because a realistic Christian faith never fails to take seriously the wrongs which are found in our human affairs, in the world in which those affairs are set, and in our own defects and failures. Genuine Christianity will have nothing to do with the easy optimism which looks at everything through rose-coloured spectacles. On the other hand, it cannot accept the total pessimism which now and again attracts us and which once found poignant expression in a phrase used by the novelist, H.G. Wells, in the period between the two world wars, when he spoke of 'the world at the end of its tether' and agreed with Bertrand Russell that 'only on the foundation of despair' can we build our human lives.

Refusing silly optimism as well as negative pessimism, Christian faith is *realistic*. It faces up to and acknowledges the evil that we all know full well; but at the same time it discerns with 'the eye of faith' that there *is* value and significance in the creation. Underneath that created world 'are the everlasting arms.' God in his love, which is the only abidingly strong power in the whole cosmos, is always there. Because he is God, his purpose cannot fail even if it may take a long time for that purpose to be accomplished in a creation to which he grants freedom to choose and responsibility to act in accordance with choices made. To have such an assurance gives us, in a very practical way, a hope that is based on something more profound than our own sentimental desires or our own cheerful wishes. It gives us confidence in life and confidence for living it. It strengthens us to do our duty and it encourages us to play our part in the struggle to overcome evil and wrong and to contribute towards the victory of righteousness and goodness. It delivers us from fears and anxieties which can gnaw away at our lives and make them miserable and ugly.

Faith discerns God

'The eye of faith' discerns God in his world; but when we try to speak about what those eyes have seen the language which is used in 'working religion' is different from that appropriate in intellectual or philosophical discourse or even in theological discussion. Certainly there is nothing wrong with the use of such theological language in the right place and at the right time. After all, we men and women are rational creatures and we think, or try to think, clearly, logically, and precisely. But in the deep things of the spirit, like human affection, appreciation of beauty, and religious life, the language which is commonly used is *not* of an intellectual, philosophical, or theological type. The language we use is the language of symbols and pictures. It is much closer to poetry which always speaks in concrete images than it is to the sort of prose which likes to use abstract idiom.

Of course some people are so unimaginative that they think that all symbolic, pictorial, or poetical language is just a pretty way of saying something that could be more accurately stated in abstract terms. Or they may have the idea that poetry is only a misrepresentation of the real facts. To their mind we get at truth when we can put things down in almost mathematical statements. For them to say things about 'the sum of the angles of a triangle' is much more factual than two people saying that they love one another very deeply and express this in such language as 'my love is like a red red rose!' They would be prepared to rely more on a chemical analysis of their friend than upon the sharing of life with that friend. So they may *say*. Of course they do not really behave in that fashion when they are actually engaged in living and not in speculating. The English poet W.H. Auden once said to me that 'poetry is always truer than prose'; yet, he added, in our modern world, so over-intellectualised in many ways and with an educational system that strongly stresses scientific approaches, it is not easy for the ordinary man or woman to recognise what in his heart of hearts he knows to be true of his experience.

The truth of pictures

I say all this because I want to insist upon the validity and importance of symbols and pictures, especially in the life of faith and in religious understanding. A famous essayist, poet, novelist, and literary critic who lived and worked in the first decades of this century was G.K. Chesterton. Chesterton was a devout Christian who wrote a number of books of apologetic in which he argued the case for Christian faith. In one of them he made a statement which puts clearly the point we are making here: 'Don't believe in anything that can't be told in painted pictures.' And the adjective 'painted' was used here by Chesterton to indicate that in religious talk there is a vivid, colourful, attractive quality like that seen in art. He was telling us that in matters of faith we are dealing with realities that can only be portrayed in just such vivid, colourful, pictorial ways.

When we consider the 'fulfilment of grace' shown in God's guarantee that the world and human existence have a value and significance more than temporary or merely temporal, we discover that the Christian tradition, in which we stand, has always used that sort of symbolical language. The tradition has spoken about the symbols of 'immortality of the soul' and 'resurrection of the body.' We must now say something about the basic meaning of those two symbols in the Christian tradition.

Immortality and resurrection

'Immortality' of the soul is not a biblical way of talking. It came into the Christian world through the influence of Hellenistic thought, an influence to which we have already referred. Its background is the specifically Hellenistic idea that each of us is essentially a 'soul' to whom bodily experiences happen but which is separable from those experiences. Thus when the human body dies, and with it there comes an end to those experiences which occur in a material world like ours, the 'soul' can continue its existence. Now, whatever may be the truth in this idea – I myself think it false – the Christian tradition has inherited from its Jewish ancestry another symbol on which it has laid much greater stress. This symbol is 'the resurrection of the body.' The point of that symbol is that human existence is not a split one, with soul on one side and body on the other; rather, it is a unified existence in which bodily experience is crucial. Therefore Christian teaching has gone on to urge that the question which really matters is what happens to us as 'body', once we are dead and the physical elements which have made up that body go 'the way of all flesh.'

When they spoke of 'body', biblical writers signified the *totality* of human life. They were building upon the Old

76

Testament story that God had taken 'the dust of the earth', had moulded it into a human form, and had then 'breathed upon it' so that it became 'a living entity.' That is the story told in Genesis about the creation of man. In due course it came to be seen that talk about 'body' in this connection was not directed simply to the chemicals and other material elements which go to make us up. The word 'body' meant *full human existence*, with such rationality, willing, and emotion as are present there. This is why the physical body as such, and as such alone, is not given *absolute* importance, although it is given genuine importance since it is necessary to our existence here and now. At death, that physical body decays. But St Paul says that 'flesh and blood cannot inherit the kingdom of God'. Hence this decaying of the physical body does not signify the utter destruction of human life; it is full human life which *can* 'inherit the kingdom of God.' St Paul affirmed that God can 'raise from the dead' a body which while *continuous with* is yet not *identical with* the physical body – it is our total personality which is raised. To phrase it in that fashion is not to use a specifically scriptural idiom, but it is to affirm what the Bible is getting at and to state it in a way that we can perhaps more readily grasp.

Human life found in God's life

This is not the place to give a further outline of the teaching which we in the Christian tradition have inherited on this subject. Suffice it to say that there is wisdom in some comments made by the contemporary American Christian thinker and writer Schubert M. Ogden of Perkins School of Theology in Dallas, Texas. Ogden has written that whatever may be the origin (and often the mistaken use) of the 'immortality of the soul' idea, it *does* at least assert the value of each personal life; and it *does* insist that God values that personal life. Hence, on the one hand, it recognises and requires us to see that each and every one of us, you and I and everyone else, has genuine significance in God's sight. On the other hand, Ogden writes, the 'resurrection of the body' idea, with its stress on our human belonging one with another in the corporate life of human society, makes equally clear that our social existence, our 'with-ness' with others of our race, and beyond that our belonging to a world of time and space and material events, are valued by God and thus have enduring significance in his sight.

Other books are readily available which discuss in detail the subject of 'the last things' – death, judgement, heaven, and hell – and which work out the Christian position on these as theology has developed over the centuries. Our concern here is not with such details, important though they are. Our concern is with understanding that through such pictorial symbols the Christian community has always declared that God's grace does indeed come to a fulfilment – and it has affirmed that such fulfilment is *in God himself*.

Our hope is in God

I have urged throughout this book that Christian faith is a theocentric or *God*-centred faith. It is not centred in *us*. It is emphatic in asserting that we are of value and significance only because God has made us more and more to become his children. To put it simply and in one sentence: our hope is to be located *in God*, not in ourselves or in our achievements. To hope in God is really to hope *in him* – it is not because by doing so we can earn or win anything, but precisely because *he, and he alone, is our hope*.

God is altogether gracious; he acts graciously towards us, with us, and in us. In his common grace he is active throughout the creation and in all human lives; in his special grace, 'the grace of our Lord Jesus Christ', he is definitively active for us and for our salvation. Because he is God, the supreme and worshipful and unsurpassable creative power, he is unexhausted and inexhaustible. His grace can never be 'used up' so that there is no more left. And because God's grace is nothing other than God's love in action, it must triumph over sin, evil, and death. Thus it is to be fulfilled. Thus also it fulfils God's creation and his children's existence. They are taken into God's own abiding life, gladly received by him, wisely used for his purposes, and given a value and significance that nothing, not even death, can destroy.

However we may think about the details of 'post-mortal' human life, whether in the language of immortality or in that of resurrection, the basic affirmation is exactly where I have sought to place it: in God himself, as by his amazing grace he comes to us and to his world, works in both, and takes both to himself, doing for both 'more than we can ask or think' and thereby granting us 'joy and peace in believing.'

8

Grace in Life Today

SUMMARY: *We prepare for the gift of grace – although we can never earn it or merit it – by being open, reverent, teachable, and dedicated people. Only those who are thus receptive are able to be 'en-graced' by God. This is why there is a necessary discipline which makes us ready to accept God's gift. It is also why God's grace must become our human task. Grace is never 'cheap'; it is always generous but also demanding of the best that we can do – however inadequate and imperfect this is bound to be.*

God's grace, God himself in his gracious activity, is a reality which every one of us experiences and knows. We may not have recognised what it is. We may not have been able to 'tag' it for what it is. We may be among those who would reject the whole business because we think ourselves to be 'hard-headed' people who have no use for religion and religious talk. Yet the divine grace is inescapably *there*, working upon us and with us and in us.

We have indicated some of the ways in which that grace acts – in the common affairs of daily life, in the natural order in the world, in general human experience, in religious sensibility wherever this is found, and supremely in the fellowship of Christian people where a response is made to God in Christ through the inspiration of God's Holy Spirit. Now, as we bring this book to a conclusion, we shall try to be very down-to-earth, very practical, and consider how, in our concrete world today, grace may, as it were, be 'lived out.' Men and women who have left their mark on the world, some of them saints and others less noticeably religious, might have been cited here; indeed, an acquaintance suggested this as a good way to end this book. But since I happen not to be fond of biographies and hence probably would not be able to make such sketches very exciting, I have preferred to do something rather different. I want to discuss simply and informally the marks of the Christian life which show how grace can be received, its 'amazing' quality expressed outwardly and known inwardly, and how the 'blessed lineaments' of Christ – to use a fine phrase from the great Bishop Thomas Wilson of Sodor and Man, so much loved by Matthew Arnold for his spiritual insight – are 'super-induced' in the Christian disciple.

First of all, though, I should like just to mention a few men and women in whom grace has evidently and wonderfully been at work. Take the case of John Newton, author of the hymn 'Amazing Grace'. In him surely grace accomplished a glorious transformation. Here was the son of a shipmaster impressed into naval service, who became a slave-trader and a man of indifferent morals. He came under the influence of the evangelical revival through meeting George Whitefield, the associate of the Wesleys. He became a different person, practically overnight. Eventually he was ordained and served first at Olney, where with his friend William Cowper he wrote many hymns which manifest a deep piety, somewhat Calvinistic in tone, like 'How sweet the name of Jesus sounds' and 'Glorious things of thee are spoken.' He became a convinced anti-slavery leader and was among those who influenced William Wilberforce in the campaign to eradicate the traffic from which originally he had profited financially.

Newton lived in the eighteenth century; he died in 1807 at the age of eighty-seven. It is a long jump backwards in history to Francis of Assisi, whose dates are 1181-1236. Yet here again grace worked marvellously to transform a young man, rich and frivolous and the darling of his home-town in Italy, into a poor, itinerant preacher of the love of God, who exhibited in his life a Christlike spirit of humility, generosity, and self-giving that won thousands back to faith and who was instrumental in effecting a reform in the life of the Church of his time. To read the story in Bonaventure's life of the saint, above all to follow him in his wanderings in Italy and the near East as these are recounted in 'The Little Flowers' which were set down by his friends after his death, is to come to know a man who has been called (with exaggeration of course) 'the only genuine Christian in the western world's history.'

In our own time, everyone has heard of the German theologian Dietrich Bonhoeffer. Brilliant as a student, effective as a teacher of German pastors, opponent of the Nazi regime in his native land, Bonhoeffer ended as a martyr to Hitler. He was put to death in a concentration camp because he persisted in his attack on the tyranny of that Nazi rule. His 'Letters from Prison' reveal a man who found strength and inward peace through dependence on divine grace. He warned his friends against what he called 'cheap grace', which meant for him polite respectability which domesticated God and forgot that God's grace was not only comfort but also demand which leads to vigorous action on behalf of justice and truth.

Again, one of my own friends was Leonard Wilson, who was captured by the Japanese during the Second World War. Wilson was missionary Bishop of Singapore, with a distinguished record of service in Christian preaching and teaching. He was a gentle and kindly man; when I knew him he had returned to Britain and soon had become

Bishop of Birmingham. Only later did I learn of the appalling torture to which he had been subjected in the Japanese prison-camp; and later still, when after his death a biography was published, I come to know that his bravery, his firm Christian witness, and his devotion even to his captors, had had the remarkable result of his later baptising and confirming several of those who had been his prison-guards and had joined in the torture inflicted on him. The sheer Christianity of the man had converted them to the Lord whom he served and by whose grace he had been sustained through his ordeal.

But these men – and women like them, such as St Theresa of Avila in Spain in the sixteenth century, her namesake Thérèse of Lisieux in France in the nineteenth century, and many others – are numbered among 'the great.' You and I are not 'great'. We are ordinary men and women who in our own time and place claim the Christian name and try to live the Christian life. What then can we say about the working of grace in our contemporary existence? Let me make a few practical suggestions about 'life in grace', appropriate to people like us.

First, we must be 'open' people – open to others, open to new ideas, ready to grasp new opportunities, and open to the working of God in our lives. The tragedy is that often enough we are just the opposite; we are 'closed' people. Far too frequently men and women who are both 'good' and 'pious' are also quite unable to see that God is continually *doing new things*, as Isaiah puts it. Their goodness is of a narrow sort and their piety is largely a matter of nostalgia for 'the old days' rather than a readiness to see the hand of God in new and perhaps disturbing events, in new knowledge about the world and human personality, in unusual and strange ideas which seem to threaten the accepted *status quo*. People like this are 'fighting the grain of the universe', said Alfred North Whitehead. Conservatism of *that* sort is negative and self-defeating; it closes us off from God's working in the world.

We need to be 'open' people; we also need to be reverent people. By this I do not necessarily mean reverent in a specifically 'religious' sense. I am thinking of how we need to be respectful, appreciative, and responsive to the world around us, to other people, and to the situations in which we find ourselves. It is very easy to be exploitative in attitude and to regard whatever is not-ourselves as there simply for our own benefit or use. It is also easy to be explorative, thinking that our job is always to investigate, enquire, or analyse that which is presented to us in experience. Sometimes we do this even with our friends and with those we love. But to be reverent means that we are prepared to see something of the wonder and glory present in life and in the world.

Robert Bridges speaks in *The Testament of Beauty* of what he calls a 'child's eyes of wonder.' We can see this in children, to be sure, to whom the world has not yet become a dull, drab, and unexciting place. We can see it also in the way some of our friends look at life. They do not so much exploit or explore; they 'expect' – in the old Latin sense of that word, meaning 'awaiting' or 'yearning' for a disclosure of the meaning hidden in mystery. It was said that Charles Darwin used to bend over his garden path and contemplate an earthworm there, with the obvious feeling that this humble creature could teach him something. Huxley said that Darwin bowed before a fact in reverence, waiting for the lesson which it had to impart to him. To be a man or woman who in his or her openness is ready to acknowledge the wonder of life – here, I believe, is another condition for our receiving grace.

The third significant point has to do with our teachability; it is obvious that this is closely related to openness and reverence. There is always a temptation to adopt the role of the talker, one who 'knows it all', one who communicates to others what he or she may in fact happen to know,

84

but is unable or unwilling to see that those others – and indeed anything and everything which we meet – have much to tell *us*. Those who have themselves been teachers know very well that one of the necessary characteristics of a good teacher is willingness to let one's students be active, not passive. A good teacher is by that very token a good listener and hence also a good learner.

Finally, a precondition for the reception of grace is the readiness to devote oneself to service of others. This may be expressed through such things as dedication to the cause of justice, readiness to work for the welfare of one's fellows in whatever way this may be possible, and willingness to give of our time and effort for the promotion of whatever is good or true or beautiful. To be 'of use' in the world: this is the point. Such delight in and devotion to service may not be easy. Often it has to be learned through the very effort it takes. Yet it can become highly rewarding in itself and bring with it a kind of concern for other people that is gratifying and satisfying. We are all of us being made for life with others; and our true happiness will be found only when we acknowledge this and act upon it. 'No man is an island, entire of itself', as John Donne tells us in a famous sermon. When we understand how true this is, and then act upon it, we are actualising something deep in our human existence. We are increasingly receptive of the common grace which is given through our relationships with others of our kind.

Now, having stressed openness, reverence, teachability, and dedication, we can move on to say something of the ways in which we are able to become more and more the conscious recipients of the divine grace as it moves towards us. This requires us to think about the practice of our religion, however inadequate that religion may be and whether it is, or is not, fully developed and mature.

The qualities which have just been mentioned do not make it possible for us either to merit or to earn the gift of God's grace. But they *do* make it possible for us to receive it. God does not act towards us in this particular fashion if we refuse all co-operation. Traditional theology has understood this when it has noted that the coming of God in Christ himself had as one of its prior conditions St Mary's willing assent, 'Be it unto me according to thy word.' She was thus the 'consentient cause of the Incarnation', as Thomas Aquinas put it. Similarly, God seeks us, invites us, and prepares the way for his coming to us; but he never forces himself upon us, so far as our conscious awareness of his presence and power is concerned.

What you and I must do, therefore, is slowly learn, through a disciplining of ourselves, to be ready for God and prepared to recognise him. In other words, it is just at this point that the importance of the practice of Christian devotion, with the several 'means' it includes, becomes apparent. I am talking of participation in the fellowship of the Christian community, the development of a life in which prayer has its place, attendance at the worship of God by the Christian congregation, and above all regular and committed presence at, and reception of, the Holy Communion. These are not optional for one who wishes earnestly to experience, consciously and directly, the reality of God's gracious activity in the very specific and heightened sense of 'the grace of our Lord Jesus Christ.' Once this has taken place, it will be possible to see intimations, hints, traces, what St Augustine called *vestigia*, of God's grace everywhere about us. One of the significant, although by no means the only significant, points of regular Christian practice in discipleship is precisely here – in providing us with a clue to what is going on in the whole of our lives. That is why William Temple could say that we call one place holy so that *all* places may be recognized as holy, one day holy so that *all* days can become holy, one meal (the Holy Communion) holy so that *all* meals can be seen as holy. It is no accident that the Church has called prayer, worship, sacrament, and devout discipleship 'means of grace.'

This is not the place to consider the 'techniques' of prayer nor the ways in which an ordered or patterned plan for worship and sacramental reception may be developed. What must be stressed, however, is that Christian discipleship is not achieved without effort and hard work. Somebody once said that 'it may not take much of a man or woman to be a Christian, but it *does* take all that such a person is.' Or, to repeat Bonhoeffer's phrase, the reality and reception of grace are never 'cheap.' They cost something; and what they cost ultimately is 'not less than a lifetime of devotion.' That last phrase is T. S. Eliot's, from *Four Quartets*; and it puts succinctly the seriousness and the demand which we dare not deny.

I have spoken of openness, reverence, teachability, and dedication to service as pre-conditions for our conscious reception of grace. I must now say that *increase* in these is a consequence of that reception. A man or woman who lives 'in grace' will be ever more open, above all to God's working; ever more reverent, above all towards the world and other people as the agencies through which that working takes places; ever more teachable, especially to what God is telling us about himself as he works in the world and in our human fellows; ever more dedicated, especially to the service of those with whom God's grace has surrounded us in our human family.

Above all, regular and faithful sharing in the life of the Christian fellowship, with its emphasis on prayer and worship and sacrament, will give 'the increase of faith, hope, and charity.' In the Prayer Book collect for the Fourteenth Sunday after Trinity, there are these fine words, 'Give unto us the increase of faith, hope, and charity; and, that we may obtain that which thou dost promise, make us to love that which thou dost command.' The word 'command' here is a translation of a Latin word which means 'the circumstances and situations in which

God's will is disclosed.' To love *these*, to accept *these* with delight, to act upon *these* to the limit of our human capacity: here, says the prayer, is how we can come to 'the increase' within us of our trust or faith, of our great expectations or hope, and of our life in love or charity. The man or woman who learns to live in faith, hope, and charity will also gladly discern 'God's gracious hand in *all* his works.'